LAW OF THE LAND

A Practical Legal Guide for Tourists and Business Travelers

UAE

By Michael L. Moore Esq.

Author: Michael L. Moore

Edited by Ally Knez-Siddique

Cover Design: Kristina Conatser

Published by: Law of the Land Publishing, LLC

ISBN: 978-1-964870-22-9

DEDICATION

This book is dedicated to the memory of my late older brother, Kenneth Lee Moore, whose tragic murder at 15 years of age inspired me to write this series of books.

This book is also dedicated to my parents, John Henry Moore, and Edna Mae Moore, whose tremendous parenting skills kept me focused on the important things in life: being reverent, getting educated, and prioritizing family.

Finally, this book is dedicated to my beautiful family, my wife, my son, and my daughter. They inspire me every single day to be kind, patient, and compassionate.

IN LOVING MEMORY OF:

Belinda Joyce Moore Moss—my beautiful and wonderful sister, who supported me in every positive thing that I ever attempted to do.

Michael Eugene Baker—my dedicated and loyal friend and brother, who always wanted the very best for me.

Sylvia Joyce Hill—my eldest sister, who had a beautiful spirit and was like a second mother to me.

PREFACE

My introduction to the justice system came when I was only 10 years old. My 15-year-old brother was murdered with a butcher knife by a 19-year-old in a simple argument over a torn shirt. I was devastated by his death and sought retribution for his fate that never came. The woman was initially charged with second degree murder, but after plea negotiations, she was convicted of manslaughter and sentenced to only five years in a youthful offender school and ordered to undergo psychiatric care. That was it. Nothing more. The judicial system had run its course.

My family knew nothing about the justice system, and we did not have the tools to advocate for ourselves. No one provided us with a written source to reference for guidance through this process. There was no easily accessible, easy to understand, definitive source to educate ourselves about the legal system that we suddenly and unexpectedly found ourselves immersed in after being victimized by such a violent criminal act.

As I got older, finished college, law school, and ultimately started practicing law, it became clear to me that most people are not knowledgeable about the law or how the judicial process works. If most people are uninformed here in the United States regarding the law and the legal process, how would they fare when in other countries? I realized that tourists and businesspeople who travel internationally needed access to information on how to navigate the legal system in other countries!

For many years, there has been considerable media attention focused on international travelers experiencing legal difficulties while traveling abroad. Most of these news stories gained attention in the United States and abroad because they involved American citizens facing punishment that was considered "unconventional" and "harsh" by United States' legal standards. I recall a news story in 1994 regarding Michael Fay, a young American male, who had broken the law in Singapore. He was convicted and sentenced to be caned and or whipped publicly. While the United States Government weighed in on the inappropriate and cruel nature of the punishment, the young American was beaten because he had been convicted under Singapore law.

Similarly, in recent years, international news stories have garnered headlines regarding foreign travelers and their issues with the laws of countries that were not their own. Amanda Knox, an American woman, was accused of murdering her roommate in Italy in 2007 and spent almost four years in an Italian prison before being definitively acquitted by the Supreme Court of Cassatio. Kenneth Bae, an American citizen, was arrested in North Korea in 2012 and was convicted for hostile acts against the communist country. He was sentenced to 15 years hard labor but was released in 2014 after efforts by the U.S. State Department. More recently, United States Basketball Star, Brittany Griner was arrested in February 2022 at a Moscow airport on drug-related charges and detained for nearly 10 months, spending much of that time in prison. Her plight unfolded at the same time Russia invaded Ukraine and further heightened tensions between Russia and the United States, ending only after she was freed in exchange for a notorious Russian arms dealer.

It was in 1994 that another personal tragic event occurred that finally inspired me to write these series of books. A dear friend and also client of mine was brutally murdered while on his second honeymoon in Jamaica. News of his murder shocked me and our local community. The legal hurdles his family had to overcome to see that justice was properly dispensed far away from home, in another country, with an entirely different set of criminal procedural rules and laws, was difficult to navigate.

As I was my friend's attorney at the time of his death, his family asked that I act as their "legal liaison" to the Jamaican Prosecutor's Office and to the Jamaican Police Department. I participated in multiple police interviews with my client's widow because she was the primary witness to his murder. As a former prosecuting attorney, I was also allowed by the Court, as a professional courtesy, to sit at the prosecutor's table to consult with the prosecuting attorney during trial. What I observed about the Jamaican trial process from a front row seat was compelling enough to cause me to seriously consider educating the "world" regarding what to expect and how to act appropriately when faced with legal issues while traveling abroad.

One of the realities in life is that, regardless of what country you are in, it is never a pleasant experience to run afoul of the law and be forced to accept that someone else will be making a decision about your pecuniary, proprietary, or penal interests (your money, your property, or your freedom).

It is important to know what the laws are, how they apply to you, and how to navigate the legal system if you are charged with a crime. It is also very helpful to know what resources are available to you if you are the victim of a criminal act. At the end of the day, an "ounce of prevention is worth a pound of cure," so the more knowledge you have, the more ammunition you possess, and the more likely you will have a positive outcome.

If you are traveling to the UAE, the first thing you should pack is a copy of this book! The helpful information and tips contained in this volume will provide a great starting point for knowing what to do (and not to do!) when you arrive at your destination and will help ensure that you have a wonderful vacation or business trip unmarred by tangles with the law.

TABLE OF CONTENTS

INTRODUCTION

IN THIS CHAPTER

- About This Book
- Hypotheticals Used Throughout This Book
- How This Book is Organized
- Icons Used in This Book
- Where to Go From Here

INTRODUCTION

As a practicing attorney for over 34 years, I have encountered numerous clients who travel often, but are unaware of the laws of the land they are traveling to.

Therefore, many years ago, I decided to write a series of books that would explain the laws of specific countries. My focus was to explain the laws that may affect travelers in a straightforward manner, without all of the legal language that is sometimes hard for even seasoned attorneys to understand.

About This Book

The aim of this book is simple. It provides you, the traveler, with a simple, easy to read book that will provide a basic legal guide that explains the law in the country that you are about to visit. It is not intended to educate you on ALL of the laws in a given country. The goal is to provide you with the details of the most common legal and safety issues faced by tourists and business travelers.

I have also provided context with background information on places not to visit, statistics on the country and prevention measures you should take to safeguard your legal and physical safety. Knowledge is a powerful thing and knowing how to stay out of trouble (or how to get out of it!) is important for everyone who travels.

This *Law of The Land/UAE* book simply helps you become more informed about your legal rights, responsibilities, and obligations in a wide range of subject areas.

Last, but not least, this book does NOT purport to offer legal advice. It does, however, provide the information you need to stay safe, follow the law and navigate around legal difficulties. However, if you do face legal difficulties, the information in this book will provide you with a starting point for solving the problem and obtaining legal assistance should it be required.

Hypotheticals Used Throughout This Book

From time to time throughout this book, I will explain the law to readers by using hypothetical scenarios. These hypotheticals will be marked by an icon that will be explained in further detail as you read on.

How This Book is Organized

CHAPTER 1: **About the UAE.** This chapter will provide you with a brief overview about the UAE and its history. It also addresses Visa requirements, monetary advice, and the best times to visit.

CHAPTER 2: **Customs.** This chapter will provide information on what to expect when entering the UAE. It will also explain what restricted and prohibited items are when entering the UAE along with custom's regulations.

CHAPTER 3: **Crime in the UAE.** This chapter provides an overview of the history of crime in the UAE and steps that UAE's officials have taken to curb the high rate of crime.

CHAPTER 4: **Criminal Law Violations.** This chapter will provide information on drug offenses, penalties, true events and questions and answers.

CHAPTER 5: **Alcohol-Related Offenses.** This chapter will provide key points regarding the sale, consumption, and regulations of alcohol use in the UAE.

CHAPTER 6: **Firearm & Ammunition Offenses.** This chapter will provide key points regarding the possession of firearms and ammunition in the UAE.

CHAPTER 7: **Prostitution.** This chapter provides an overview of the history of prostitution in the UAE, laws and penalties, prostitution practices, sex trafficking, sex tourism, health in the UAE, tips to avoid being hassled, a Law of the Land Hypothetical, and the current situation on prostitution in the UAE.

CHAPTER 8: **LGBTQ.** This chapter will provide information regarding the acceptance of LGBTQ people in the UAE and the laws surrounding homosexuality.

CHAPTER 9: **Sexually Motivated/Violent Crimes.** This chapter will provide an overview of sexually related crimes in the UAE.

CHAPTER 10: **Arrested in the UAE.** This chapter will provide information on what to do if you are arrested in the UAE.

CHAPTER 11: **Jails vs. Prisons: Conditions & Culture.** This chapter will provide information on the conditions and culture of the UAE's Jails and Prisons.

CHAPTER 12: **Helping a Friend or Relative Imprisoned in the UAE.** This chapter will provide information on how you can assist a friend or relative imprisoned in the UAE.

CHAPTER 13: **The Administration of Justice.** This chapter will provide information on the UAE's Legal System.

CHAPTER 14: **Crime Victim Assistance.** This chapter will provide information on crime victim assistance along with providing safety tips.

CHAPTER 15: **Police.** This chapter will provide information on the UAE's Police and how to report a crime.

CHAPTER 16: **How to Get Legal Help in the UAE.** This chapter will provide information regarding how to obtain legal assistance for travelers to the UAE.

CHAPTER 17: **Medical Facilities & Hospitals.** This chapter will provide information about how to obtain medical care while visiting the UAE.

CHAPTER 18: **Driving in the UAE.** This chapter will provide information on driving in the UAE, it's traffic rules, and road safety tips.

CHAPTER 19: **Nude Beaches & Clothing-Optional Resorts.** This chapter will provide an overview of nude beaches and clothing-optional resorts in the UAE, and the legality and safety of visiting nude beaches in the UAE.

CHAPTER 20: **Unusual Laws.** This chapter will provide information on some Unusual Laws in the UAE, and penalties and fines.

CHAPTER 21: **Traveling Safely.** This chapter will provide information on women traveling alone, crime prevention for families, safety notes for all travelers, and overall advice.

CHAPTER 22: **Tourist Taxation.** This chapter will provide information on taxes that tourists are required to pay in the UAE.

CHAPTER 23: **Long-Term Stays.** This chapter will provide an overview of the consequences for overstaying your visit to the UAE.

CHAPTER 24: **Civil Litigation.** This chapter will provide information about the civil litigation process in the UAE.

CHAPTER 25: **Other Things to Know.** This chapter will provide information on the harassment of tourists, travel and safety, and other practical tips.

CHAPTER 26: **Quick Reference Guide.** This chapter is a quick way to get information. It is a condensed version of the chapters in this book.

Emergency/Important Contact Numbers in the UAE

Useful Arabic Phrases

Glossary

Icons Used in this Book

What do those pictures throughout the book mean? See below:

WARNING: This icon flags information about things you should **avoid** while visiting the UAE. Heed the advice next to this icon to avoid legal perils.

REMEMBER: This icon flags noteworthy information that you **shouldn't forget**.

HELPFUL TIPS: This icon flags information that will help you when entering the UAE, relates to a legal situation, or refers to resources available while visiting the UAE.

TECHNICAL INFORMATION: This icon flags technical aspects of the law. If you are faced with a legal problem, and you want to learn more about the law involved, this information can be helpful.

ADDITIONAL INFORMATION: This icon points to the location of additional information available on the internet.

HYPOTHETICAL: This icon points to hypothetical scenarios to illustrate possible legal problems and the outcome.

QUESTIONS: This icon points to questions and answers throughout the book.

TRUE STORY: This icon points to true events throughout the book.

Where to Go From Here

If you have a specific question about the law in the UAE as it relates to a particular area, just turn to the chapter that addresses that issue, or turn to the Quick Reference Guide. You can also read the book from cover to cover to obtain a more comprehensive understanding of the UAE's laws and resources available should you find yourself in a legal predicament while visiting.

Disclaimer: While the recommendations in this book primarily address U.S. citizens, the information is relevant and applicable to citizens of any country.

CHAPTER 1

ABOUT THE UAE

IN THIS CHAPTER

- About the UAE
- UAE, the Basics
- UAE's Hospitality

CHAPTER 1

ABOUT THE UAE

About the UAE

The United Arab Emirates is located in the **southeastern region of the Arabian Peninsula**, bordering Saudi Arabia to the south and west and Oman to the southeast. It has a long coastline along the Persian Gulf and is strategically positioned near the Strait of Hormuz—a key global oil route. Covering about **83,600 square kilometers (32,278 square miles)**, the UAE is relatively small in geographic size, especially compared to its regional neighbors. As of 2024, the UAE has a population of approximately **9.5 million people**, though **only about 11–12% are Emirati citizens**; the rest are expatriates from countries like India, Pakistan, the Philippines, Egypt, and the UK.

The UAE is best known for its **luxury lifestyle, ultramodern architecture, desert landscapes, and futuristic cities** like Dubai and Abu Dhabi. It is a major global hub for **business, tourism, and aviation**, and has become synonymous with **iconic landmarks** such as the **Burj Khalifa (the tallest building in the world)**, **Palm Jumeirah**, and the **Louvre Abu Dhabi.** With vast oil reserves and a rapidly diversifying economy, the UAE blends **traditional Islamic culture** with **cosmopolitan modernity**, drawing visitors and investors from around the world.

The UAE was formed in **1971** when seven emirates—**Abu Dhabi, Dubai, Sharjah, Ajman, Umm Al-Quwain, Fujairah**, and later **Ras Al Khaimah**—united to form a single federation after British protection over the region ended. Before unification, the area was known as the **Trucial States**, and its economy was centered on **pearling, fishing, and trade.** However, since independence, the UAE has undergone a **remarkable transformation**—from a series of desert settlements into one of the most advanced and affluent nations in the Middle East. Spearheaded by visionary leaders like **Sheikh Zayed bin Sultan Al Nahyan**, the founding father and first president, the country invested heavily in infrastructure, education, and international partnerships. Today, the UAE is known for its **stability, global influence, and rapid development**, serving as a bridge between East and West.

The Capital

Abu Dhabi is the capital of the UAE and its largest emirate by land area. Located on an island in the Persian Gulf, Abu Dhabi serves as the **political, industrial, and cultural center** of the country. It is also home to the federal government, the Presidential Palace, and most of the country's oil wealth.

The city is known for its sleek skyscrapers, palm-lined boulevards, and cultural institutions. Highlights include the **Sheikh Zayed Grand Mosque**, a marvel of Islamic architecture, and **Louvre Abu Dhabi**, an art museum that symbolizes the country's openness to global culture. Abu Dhabi offers a more reserved, traditional atmosphere compared to glitzy Dubai but is equally ambitious in vision, especially with its sustainability-focused **Masdar City project** and upcoming **Guggenheim museum.**

The People

The native citizens of the UAE are known as **Emiratis.** However, they make up only a small portion of the population, as the country relies heavily on foreign labor and talent. Emiratis are known for their **hospitality, pride in tradition, and strong family values.** Despite the modern, fast-paced lifestyle of cities like Dubai, many Emiratis maintain a deep connection to **Bedouin heritage, Islamic customs**, and **tribal roots.**

The UAE's multicultural society includes a vast range of ethnicities, religions, and languages, especially in its larger cities. Expatriates, especially from South Asia, Southeast Asia, and Europe, form the backbone of the UAE's workforce and have contributed significantly to its economic success.

Language

The official language of the UAE is **Arabic**, and it is used in government, media, and education. However, **English is widely spoken**, especially in business, tourism, and day-to-day interactions. Due to its large expatriate population, the UAE is also home to many speakers of **Hindi, Urdu, Malayalam, Tagalog, Farsi, and other languages**. Road signs, menus, and government documents are usually bilingual (Arabic and English), and English-language media is abundant. Most residents, especially in Dubai and Abu Dhabi, are at least conversational in English.

Religion

Islam is the official religion of the UAE, and it deeply influences the country's laws, culture, and daily life. The majority of Emiratis are **Sunni Muslims**, although there is also a significant **Shiite minority**. Islamic values are reflected in everything from **dress codes and public behavior** to **holiday observances** like **Ramadan** and **Eid.**

That said, the UAE is known for its **religious tolerance**. It allows people of other faiths to **worship freely**. Cities like Dubai and Abu Dhabi are home to churches, Hindu temples, Sikh gurdwaras, and even a newly opened synagogue, part of the Abrahamic Family House—a multi-faith complex meant to promote interfaith harmony.

Affordability

The cost of living in the UAE **varies greatly** depending on the emirate and your lifestyle. **Dubai** and **Abu Dhabi** tend to be **more expensive**, while emirates like Sharjah and Ajman are more **affordable** for housing and daily expenses.

For example, monthly rent for a one-bedroom apartment in Dubai's city center can range from **$1,500 USD–$2,500 USD**, while in Sharjah or Ajman it might be **$700 USD–$1,200 USD.**

Eating out can be affordable or luxurious. A basic meal at a local restaurant may cost **$7 USD–$12 USD**, while a three-course dinner at a mid-range restaurant could run **$30 USD–$50 USD.** Groceries are reasonably priced, especially if you stick to local markets and avoid imported goods.

Public transit is **clean and affordable.** In Dubai, a metro ride costs **$0.80 USD–$2.00 USD**, and a monthly pass is around **$80–$100.** Gasoline is cheap by global standards, averaging around **$0.80 USD per liter** (**$3.00 USD per gallon**) due to domestic oil subsidies.

Many of the UAE's top attractions—like **beaches, mosques, and shopping malls**—are free or low-cost. Entry to major landmarks like the **Burj Khalifa observation deck** ranges from **$40 USD–$100 USD**, depending on the time and package. Desert safaris, water parks, and yacht cruises typically range from **$50 USD–$150 USD.**

UAE, the Basics

How to get there?

The UAE is one of the **most accessible and well-connected destinations in the Middle East**, serving as a **major transit and tourism hub** between Europe, Asia, Africa, and the Americas. It offers a wide range of flight options, including full-service and budget airlines, with extensive international connections. Thanks to its strategic location and world-class airport infrastructure, getting to the UAE is straightforward from virtually anywhere in the world.

Major International Airports in the UAE include:

- **Dubai International Airport** (**DXB**): Located in Dubai, DXB is the **busiest airport in the world by international passenger traffic.**

It serves as the primary gateway to the UAE and a major hub for **Emirates**, the country's flagship airline. DXB offers **direct flights from hundreds of global cities**, including major U.S., European, Asian, and African destinations. The airport is known for its state-of-the-art facilities, excellent shopping, and efficient connections.

- **Abu Dhabi International Airport (AUH):** Serving the capital city, AUH is the **second-largest airport in the UAE**. It is a hub for **Etihad Airways**, the national airline of the UAE. Etihad operates long-haul flights to **North America, Europe, Asia, and Australia.** The airport is currently being expanded with the opening of the new **Terminal A** to accommodate increased traffic and offer faster transit.
- **Sharjah International Airport (SHJ):** Located near Dubai, this airport is a growing hub for low-cost carriers, especially **Air Arabia**, the UAE's leading budget airline. It offers affordable connections to **South Asia, Central Asia, North Africa, and Eastern Europe**, making it popular among cost-conscious travelers.
- **Al Maktoum International Airport (DWC):** Also known as **Dubai World Central**, DWC is a newer airport located in the southern part of Dubai. While it currently handles fewer passenger flights, it is expected to become one of the world's largest airports as it expands. It primarily serves cargo and seasonal traffic but is growing in importance.

The UAE is a key hub for many **international airlines**. Top carriers include:

- **Emirates (based in Dubai):** Offers direct flights to over 130 destinations, including major cities in the U.S. (New York, Los Angeles, Chicago, Dallas, Houston, Boston, Miami, Orlando, Seattle, San Francisco), Canada (Toronto), UK, Europe, Asia, Africa, and Oceania.
- **Etihad Airways (based in Abu Dhabi):** Flies directly to cities like New York, Chicago, Washington D.C., Toronto, London, Paris, Frankfurt, Mumbai, Tokyo, and Sydney.
- **Qatar Airways, Turkish Airlines, British Airways, Lufthansa, Air France, KLM, Singapore Airlines, and Saudia** all operate regular flights into DXB and AUH.

- **United Airlines, Delta Air Lines, and American Airlines** codeshare with Emirates and Etihad for smooth U.S. connections.
- Budget options like **Air Arabia, flydubai**, and **Wizz Air Abu Dhabi** offer affordable regional and short-haul flights across Asia, Europe, and the Middle East.

Flights to the UAE vary in cost depending on the season, airline, and departure city. Generally, the **low season** is from **June to August**, when the UAE experiences extreme summer heat with temperatures often exceeding 105°F (40°C). This period is the cheapest time to fly, especially from Europe, Asia, and North America. Round-trip fares from U.S. cities can drop as low as $600 to $800 USD, particularly if booked well in advance.

The **shoulder season**, from **March to May** and **September to early November**, offer more pleasant weather and still reasonable fares. Prices during these months typically range from $800 to $1,000 USD for round-trip flights from North America. **High season** occurs from **late November to February** when the weather is most comfortable. This is the peak tourism period, and flights tend to be more expensive, with fares from the U.S. often exceeding $1,200 USD for round-trip tickets unless booked several months ahead.

Additionally, global events such as **Expo Dubai, New Year's celebrations**, or the **Abu Dhabi Grand Prix** can cause fares to rise during specific times. For the best deals, it's helpful to use fare comparison tools like Google Flights, Skyscanner, or Hopper, be flexible with travel dates, and consider flying into Abu Dhabi (AUH) or Sharjah (SHJ) airports as alternatives to Dubai International (DXB).

When to Visit?

The best time to visit the UAE depends on your preferences for weather, crowds, and activities. The country has a desert climate with very hot summers and mild winters. The peak tourist season runs from November to March, when temperatures are comfortable—usually between the mid-70s and mid-80s°F (24–30°C)—ideal for outdoor activities like desert safaris, beach outings, and sightseeing.

The off-season is during the summer months, June to September, when temperatures often exceed 100°F (38°C). This period sees fewer tourists due to the extreme heat, but it offers lower prices on flights and hotels. Many visitors use this time to enjoy indoor attractions like shopping malls, luxury resorts, and indoor ski facilities.

The shoulder seasons in April, May, and October provide warm but manageable weather and fewer crowds, making them good alternatives if you want to avoid the busiest times.

The UAE hosts several famous events throughout the year. The Dubai Shopping Festival in January and February features huge discounts and entertainment. The Abu Dhabi Grand Prix in November draws motorsport fans worldwide. National Day on December 2 celebrates the country's formation with parades and fireworks. Islamic holidays like Eid al-Fitr and Eid al-Adha are celebrated with public festivities and special events, although their dates change each year. Visiting during these festivals offers rich cultural experiences but also larger crowds and higher prices.

ADDITIONAL INFORMATION

Do I Need a Visa?

Visa requirements for visiting the UAE vary depending on your nationality, length of stay, and the purpose of your visit. Citizens of many countries, including the **United States, Canada, the United Kingdom, Australia**, and **most European nations**, are eligible for a **visa on arrival** at the UAE airports. This visa typically allows for a stay of **up to 30 days** and can often be extended once for an additional 30 days.

Travelers from countries not eligible for visa on arrival must apply for a visa in advance through a UAE embassy, consulate, or via the official e-visa platform. Tourist visas generally come in **30-day** or **90-day validity options**, with single-entry or multiple-entry possibilities depending on the visa type and issuing authority. However, if you plan to visit for purposes other than tourism—such as work, study, or long-term residence—you will need to apply for the appropriate visa or residency permit prior to entering the UAE. These visas require sponsorship, usually from an employer, educational institution, or family member residing in the UAE.

It is important to check the most current visa policies before traveling, as regulations can change frequently. Official UAE government websites and local embassies provide the most accurate and up-to-date information on visa eligibility, application procedures, and fees.

How to Get Around

Getting around the United Arab Emirates as a tourist is generally easy and efficient, thanks to its modern infrastructure and wide range of transportation options. **Taxis** are one of the most convenient choices for short trips and are widely available in all major cities, especially Dubai and Abu Dhabi. They are metered, air-conditioned, and relatively affordable by international standards. You can hail a cab on the street or use ride-hailing apps like **Careem**, **Uber**, or the **Dubai Taxi Corporation** app, all of which support English and allow for cashless payments.

Dubai has a highly efficient **metro system** that connects key locations such as the airport, major malls, and tourist hotspots like the Marina and Downtown Dubai. The metro is clean, fast, and inexpensive, with fares ranging from about $0.80 to $2.50 USD per ride, depending on distance. Passengers use a **Nol card** for access, which also works on trams, buses, and water transport in Dubai. However, public transportation coverage beyond Dubai is limited, as cities like Abu Dhabi and Sharjah do not have metro systems. Instead, they rely more on buses and taxis.

If you're planning to explore areas outside the main cities—such as deserts, beaches, or the mountainous regions of Fujairah—**renting a car** is a good option. Rental rates start at around $30 USD per day, and an international driving permit or a license from certain countries is required. The highways are modern and well-signposted, but drivers should be aware of toll roads (like Dubai's Salik system) and often confusing city traffic patterns. Parking is usually available but may come with fees.

Intercity travel between emirates is well-supported by **budget-friendly buses** operated by systems like **Emirates Express** and the **RTA**. Popular routes such as Dubai to Abu Dhabi or Dubai to Sharjah cost around $2 to $6 USD and are air-conditioned and safe. These buses can take longer than driving, especially during peak hours, but they're a solid option for budget-conscious travelers.

For a more scenic experience, Dubai offers several types of **water transport**. Traditional **abras** ferry passengers across Dubai Creek for as little as $0.30 USD, while water buses and ferries offer longer, more relaxed routes across the coastlines for slightly higher prices. These options not only provide an affordable way to travel but also a unique view of the city's architecture and history.

Walking and cycling are viable in select areas like Downtown Dubai, the Jumeirah Corniche, and the Abu Dhabi Corniche, but the summer heat from May through September can make both options uncomfortable. That said, Dubai has made recent improvements in its cycling infrastructure, and services like Careem Bike allow for short-term rentals, especially in cooler months.

Monetary Advice

When traveling in the United Arab Emirates, it's important to understand how money works to avoid confusion and make the most of your experience.

The national currency is the **UAE dirham**, abbreviated as **AED**. One dirham is divided into 100 fils. The exchange rate is generally stable, with **1 USD equal to approximately 3.67 AED**. You can exchange money at banks, currency exchange offices, airports, and shopping malls. Exchange counters in malls and city centers usually offer better rates than those at airports or hotels. ATMs are widely available and typically offer good exchange rates, though your bank at home may charge international withdrawal fees.

Credit and debit cards are **widely accepted** throughout the UAE, especially in cities like Dubai and Abu Dhabi. Visa and Mastercard are the most commonly accepted, while American Express and others may be accepted at higher-end establishments. Cash is still useful for small purchases, local markets, and in more remote areas. While you can sometimes pay in other currencies like US dollars, British pounds, or euros at major tourist spots or hotel resorts, these payments are not common, and the exchange rate offered is usually less favorable. It's best to pay in dirhams whenever possible.

Bargaining is **part of the shopping culture** in **traditional markets** known as *souks*, such as the Gold Souk or Spice Souk in Dubai. In these settings, haggling is expected and even encouraged. Start by offering about half the asking price and negotiate respectfully from there. However, in malls, supermarkets, and fixed-price stores, prices are **non-negotiable**, and bargaining would be inappropriate.

Tipping in the UAE is **not obligatory**, but it is appreciated. In restaurants, it's common to leave a tip of **5% to 10%**, especially if service is not already included in the bill. For taxi drivers, rounding up to the nearest dirham or leaving a small tip of **2 to 5 AED** is customary. Hotel staff such as porters and valet attendants typically receive **5 to 10 AED**, depending on the level of service. At spas or salons, a **10% tip** is also standard if you're satisfied with the service.

The UAE's Hospitality

The United Arab Emirates is known for its legendary hospitality, which is deeply rooted in **Bedouin traditions** and reinforced by **Islamic values** of generosity, respect, and community. Visitors often find the country striking not only for its futuristic skyline and luxury shopping, but also for how warmly they are welcomed by locals and residents alike.

Hospitality in the UAE is expressed through acts of **generosity**, such as offering guests Arabic coffee (*gahwa*), dates, and sometimes even meals—especially during cultural celebrations or visits to Emirati homes. You might be greeted with a warm handshake or the phrase "*Ahlan wa sahlan*" (welcome), and it is common for hosts to go out of their way to make sure guests feel comfortable and well taken care of. In more formal or traditional settings, such as majlis gatherings (a space for social and political meetings), guests are seated according to seniority and offered refreshments, reflecting a deep respect for etiquette.

Politeness in the UAE is demonstrated through **modesty, patience, and respectful language**. Always greet people with "*As-salamu alaykum*" (peace be upon you), especially in traditional settings. Using your right hand for handshakes, eating, or giving items is considered polite, as the left hand is traditionally viewed as unclean. Public displays of affection, loud behavior, and swearing are frowned upon and can even result in fines or legal issues. It's also important to dress modestly in public—women should aim to cover their shoulders and knees, while men should avoid wearing sleeveless shirts or very short shorts outside the beach or pool area.

As a visitor, showing respect for Emirati culture means being mindful of both laws and social customs. During the holy month of Ramadan, for example, eating, drinking, or smoking in public during daylight hours should be avoided, even by non-Muslims. Visiting mosques requires appropriate attire, including headscarves for women and long pants for all visitors. Taking photos of people, especially women, without permission is also considered disrespectful. On the other hand, showing interest in local traditions, trying Emirati cuisine, or learning a few Arabic phrases is often appreciated and seen as a gesture of goodwill.

CHAPTER 2

CUSTOMS

IN THIS CHAPTER

- Travelers Entering the UAE
- Customs Entitlements and Monetary Restrictions
- Restricted and Prohibited Items
- Five Practical Tips to Know Before You Go

CHAPTER 2

CUSTOMS

Travelers Entering the UAE

To enter the United Arab Emirates (UAE), travelers must carry a passport that is valid for at least six months from the date of entry and has at least two blank pages for visa stamps. Depending on your nationality, you may be eligible for a **visa on arrival**, a **pre-arranged tourist visa**, or a **transit visa**. U.S. citizens, for example, can obtain a 30-day visa on arrival free of charge, which is extendable. Citizens from many European and Asian countries are also eligible for visa-free entry or visa-on-arrival privileges. Indian citizens holding a valid U.S. visa, green card, or residency in the EU/UK may obtain a 14-day visa on arrival for a small fee. Travelers from countries not on the visa-on-arrival list must apply in advance for an e-visa through an airline, hotel, UAE embassy, or the official government portal.

When entering the country, all travelers should carry their passport, confirmed return or onward ticket, proof of accommodation (such as a hotel booking or sponsor details), and, if applicable, a printed or digital copy of their visa. Travel insurance is not mandatory but is highly recommended, especially for medical coverage.

Upon landing in the UAE, expect standard arrival procedures including immigration checks, visa stamping, and baggage claim. In major airports like Dubai and Abu Dhabi, travelers might be asked for a printed visa or passport copy, especially at random visual security checkpoints—there is a small fee if you need to print at the airport. Travelers eligible for Smart Gates may use them to expedite immigration. Medical exams are only required if you are entering on a residence or work visa, not for tourists.

For updated travel advisories, you can check the official UAE government portal at **u.ae**, your airline's travel requirements page, and for U.S. citizens, the U.S. State Department's travel page at **travel.state.gov**. These sites provide the most current information on visa requirements, health advisories, and safety recommendations.

Customs Entitlements and Monetary Restrictions

There are restrictions on currency and goods when entering the United Arab Emirates (UAE), and travelers should be aware of these to avoid fines, confiscation, or legal issues. In terms of currency, travelers entering or leaving the UAE **must declare amounts over 60,000 AED** (approximately $16,300 USD), including cash, traveler's checks, precious metals, or negotiable instruments. This rule applies to adults and minors individually, though minors' declarations must be made by an accompanying adult. Undeclared large sums may be confiscated under anti-money laundering laws.[1]

Regarding goods, travelers are allowed to bring in personal items and gifts valued **up to 3,000 AED (about $820 USD)** without customs duties. There are specific allowances for **tobacco** (400 cigarettes, 50 cigars, 500g of tobacco) and **alcohol** (up to 4 liters or 2 cartons of beer for non-Muslim adults). **Medicines** can be brought in small quantities for personal use, but certain medications—especially those considered narcotic or psychotropic—require prior approval from the Ministry of Health. It's essential to carry the original prescription and packaging.

1 https://www.dubaicustoms.gov.ae/en/Individuals/CustomsGuide/Pages/TravellerCustomsGuide.aspx

Travelers should always declare large sums of money and carry documentation for medications. Customs inspection is routine, and non-compliance may lead to confiscation, penalties, or deportation.

Restricted and Prohibited Items

Travelers entering the UAE should be aware that certain items are strictly prohibited, while others are restricted and require prior permission. **Prohibited items** include **narcotic drugs, gambling devices, counterfeit goods, materials related to black magic or sorcery, any publications or artworks that contradict Islamic values, radioactive or contaminated substances, reconditioned tires, paan and betel leaves, and various types of offensive or obscene media.** These items are banned outright and cannot be brought into the country under any circumstances.

Restricted items can be brought into the UAE only with advance approval from the relevant authorities. This category includes **medications and medical equipment, firearms and ammunition, explosives, live animals, plants, fertilizers, alcohol, wireless communication devices, electronic cigarettes, cosmetics, and raw diamonds**. These goods are regulated by multiple UAE government agencies such as the Ministry of Health, Ministry of Interior, Ministry of Climate Change and Environment, and the Telecommunications and Digital Government Regulatory Authority. Travelers should apply for the necessary permits before bringing in any of these goods.

If a traveler attempts to bring prohibited items into the country, those goods will be **confiscated** immediately, and the individual **may face serious consequences**. Depending on the severity of the offense, consequences can include heavy fines, imprisonment, deportation, and long-term or permanent travel bans. Bringing restricted items without the proper permits can also lead to penalties, though in some cases it may result in fines or legal warnings if deemed a minor violation.

Medications are a particularly sensitive category. Travelers are required to carry a valid doctor's prescription, preferably in English or Arabic, and must bring medicines in their original packaging. If the medication contains controlled substances, travelers must obtain prior approval through the UAE Ministry of Health and Prevention's online portal. Carrying restricted medications without authorization can result in arrest, prosecution, and steep financial penalties.

To avoid issues at the border, travelers should consult the official UAE customs website for the most up-to-date list of prohibited and restricted items at **www.customs.gov.ae** or use the UAE government portal at **www.u.ae.** When in doubt, it is always safer to declare the item or request approval in advance.

Five Practical Tips to Know Before You Go

1. **Dress modestly in public spaces:** Both men and women should wear clothing that covers shoulders and knees, especially in malls, mosques, and government offices. Swimwear is only acceptable at beaches and hotel pools.
2. **Limit public displays of affection:** Holding hands is generally acceptable for married couples, but kissing or hugging in public is frowned upon and can result in fines or warnings.
3. **Use your right hand:** Always eat, greet, and pass items using your right hand. The left hand is considered impolite for these interactions in Emirati culture.
4. **Be respectful during Ramadan and in homes:** Do not eat, drink, or smoke in public during daylight hours in Ramadan. When offered Arabic coffee or dates, accept with your right hand and gently shake the cup when finished.
5. **Be mindful of local laws and behavior:** Avoid swearing, making rude gestures, taking photos of people without permission, or posting anything critical of the UAE government online or in person. These actions can lead to serious legal consequences.

CHAPTER 3

CRIME IN THE UAE

IN THIS CHAPTER

- Overview
- Crime Hotspots in the UAE
- Crime Statistics
- Quick Safety Tips

CHAPTER 3

CRIME IN THE UAE

Overview

The UAE is widely regarded as **extremely safe**, with very low crime levels by international standards. Global surveys consistently rank the country among the world's safest. For example, *Numbeo's 2025 Safety Index* lists the UAE as the second safest nation globally (safety score 84.5) and the second lowest on its crime index. Petty street crimes (pickpocketing, mugging, etc.) are *uncommon*, and violent crime is extremely rare. Indeed, the country's homicide rate has been well under 1 per 100,000 people for years versus a global average of about 5.6 per 100,000 people.[2]

Several factors underlie the UAE's low crime levels. **Strict laws and enforcement** are primary drivers: drug use, theft, sexual offenses and many other crimes carry severe penalties (often lengthy prison terms or even death for the most serious drug and violent crimes). Law enforcement is robust – police forces in each emirate are well-funded, technologically advanced, and highly visible. For example, Dubai and Abu Dhabi police have adopted AI-based "predictive policing" and extensive CCTV networks to prevent and solve crimes.[3] The U.S. government travel advisory explicitly warns that the UAE has **"strict rules on social behavior, drug possession, traffic violations, and financial crimes"** and that breaking these laws can result in arrest or deportation.

2 macrotrends.neten.wikipedia.org

3 khaleejtimes.com

Other influences on crime include the UAE's **economy and demographics.** The country is very wealthy (high GDP per capita) and invests heavily in public services and social stability. While there are income disparities (and many low-paid migrant workers), outright poverty is rare and social welfare for citizens is strong. Additionally, family and community networks are often strong, and cultural norms (including conservative social values) further discourage street crime. In short, a combination of **economic prosperity, a large and disciplined police force, harsh legal penalties, and social cohesion** contribute to the UAE's low crime

Crime Hotspots in the UAE

The United Arab Emirates is widely regarded as one of the safest countries in the world, and this holds true for both tourists and residents across all seven emirates. Most of the country, including the central and affluent districts of Dubai, Abu Dhabi, and Sharjah, is considered very safe with extremely low rates of violent and non-violent crime. Areas such as Downtown Dubai, Dubai Marina, the Palm Jumeirah, Business Bay, and DIFC are heavily monitored by security personnel and CCTV, making them particularly safe for tourists. In Abu Dhabi, similarly secure areas include the Corniche, Saadiyat Island, Yas Island, and Al Maryah Island. In Sharjah, the Al Majaz waterfront and University City also enjoy strong reputations for safety.

That said, a few areas are considered to have **higher exposure to petty crime** such as pickpocketing, scams, or minor theft, especially in crowded places. In **Dubai, Naif and Al Sabkha in the Deira district**—home to bustling souks and older transportation hubs—were historically known for such incidents, though increased policing and surveillance have significantly reduced problems there. **Satwa**, another mixed-use neighborhood, had a similar reputation in the past. Additionally, **Sonapur (Muhaisnah 2)**, a labor housing district in Dubai, is not unsafe in the traditional sense but is overcrowded and lacks the infrastructure for visitors, making it unsuitable for tourists. In **Abu Dhabi, Mussafah Industrial Zone** shares similar characteristics. In **Sharjah, the 18 industrial areas**—including Al Sajja—and the **city center** at night are more prone to petty theft and are best approached with caution after dark, especially by solo travelers.

Tourists are advised to **avoid labor camps** entirely, such as those in Sonapur, Jebel Ali, and Sharjah's industrial zones. These areas are not tourist destinations and have been linked with occasional thefts or disputes, mainly among laborers. While violent crime remains extremely rare, crowded bus terminals and older market areas can be hotspots for opportunistic theft, particularly after dark. Visitors should also be mindful in poorly lit industrial zones at night, which, while not inherently dangerous, can be disorienting and poorly secured.

Before traveling, it's always a good idea to check **official travel advisories** from your home country.

Crime Statistics

Crime in the UAE remains remarkably low by global standards, and the country is widely considered one of the safest in the world. Both violent and non-violent crimes occur at minimal rates, and most criminal activity is limited to petty theft, fraud, and cybercrime. The most common offenses include **pickpocketing** in crowded areas like traditional markets, beaches, or public transport systems. Vehicle break-ins are rare, but tourists should still avoid leaving valuables visible inside cars. **Fraud** and **digital scams**, such as phishing emails, ATM skimming, and SIM-swap fraud, have become more widespread in recent years, with authorities and banks issuing public warnings. A notable case involved over 47 million AED ($12.8 million USD) lost to SIM-swap fraud, and Visa has reported that up to 90% of UAE residents are vulnerable to digital scams. **Cybercrime** is a growing concern as well, targeting individuals and businesses through malware and hacking, prompting the establishment of dedicated cybercrime units and new legislation. While **financial** and **drug-related crimes** do exist—particularly involving international smuggling and money laundering—the UAE's harsh penalties and strong enforcement limit domestic activity. In 2019, Dubai police seized over $1 billion worth of illegal drugs, underscoring their vigilance. Incidents involving tourists are infrequent, and when they occur, they are usually non-violent, such as theft or scams.

Occasional cases of sexual harassment or inappropriate behavior have been reported, but these are dealt with swiftly by law enforcement. For tourists, the most likely risks involve petty crime or falling victim to online scams, particularly when booking accommodations or excursions through unofficial websites. While physical safety is not a major concern, travelers are still advised to take basic precautions such as avoiding poorly lit areas at night, watching their belongings in busy markets, and using reputable vendors and service providers.

Quick Safety Tips

- The UAE has strict laws regarding public behavior, dress, alcohol, and relationships. Avoid public displays of affection, dress modestly in public areas (especially in malls and religious sites), and never use offensive language or gestures. What might be minor infractions elsewhere can lead to fines, detention, or deportation in the UAE.
- Although crime is rare, petty theft such as pickpocketing can still occur in busy places like markets, beaches, or metro stations. Always keep valuables close, avoid flashing cash or expensive items, and use hotel safes when possible.
- Taking pictures of Emiratis, especially women, without permission is not only disrespectful but can lead to legal trouble. It is also prohibited to photograph government buildings, military sites, and airports.
- Stick to official taxis (often cream-colored with a regulated meter) or use reliable ride-hailing apps like Uber or Careem. Avoid accepting rides from unlicensed drivers.
- Rules can change quickly, especially concerning drugs, medications, and electronic communications. Some over-the-counter medications in other countries are banned in the UAE. Always

check with the UAE embassy or consulate before traveling with prescription meds and review current travel advisories.

- Disputes, yelling, or aggressive behavior—even online—can be reported as harassment or defamation. Stay calm and polite in all public and private interactions. UAE law emphasizes respect and public order, and violations can result in fines or arrest.

CHAPTER 4

CRIMINAL LAW VIOLATIONS

IN THIS CHAPTER

- Marijuana and Other Drugs in the UAE
- Prescription Medication
- General Questions
- Law of the Land True Story
- Takeaways

CHAPTER 4

CRIMINAL LAW VIOLATIONS

Marijuana and Other Drugs in the UAE

The UAE enforces some of the world's **strictest drug laws**, applying a **zero-tolerance approach to cannabis, synthetic cannabinoids, and all other narcotics.** Historically, even trace amounts of cannabis—whether smoked abroad or lingering on clothing—could result in imprisonment of up to four years, especially when detected via blood or urine tests at ports of entry.[4] In 2012, the UAE became the first Arab country to formally classify **synthetic cannabinoids** (e.g., Spice, K2) as **Schedule I substances**, banning over 50 variants; these are subject to the same or even harsher penalties than natural cannabis.

In November 2021, **Federal Decree Law No. 30 of 2021** introduced reforms that eased consequences for first-time personal use offenders. Now, possession of small amounts—including imported THC-containing food or drinks—may result only in **confiscation and destruction of the substance**, not imprisonment. However, **possessing or using cannabis**—including CBD oil—is **still illegal** and can result in a sentence of **three months to four years**, along with hefty fines. Repeat offenses within three years escalate to a minimum of six months in prison and even more significant fines; a third offense carries at least two years in jail and fines of 100,000 AED (about $27,230 USD) or more.[5]

4 https://hzlegal.ae/drugs-and-the-law-in-dubai

5 https://wirestork.com/dubai-law-on-dugs

"Classic" illicit drugs—cocaine, heroin, LSD, methamphetamines—fall under Category 1 and carry minimum **four-year prison sentences** plus fines of at least **20,000 AED (roughly $5,445 USD)** for possession. Trafficking these substances may result in **life imprisonment**, fines **up to 200,000 AED (around $54,450 USD)**, deportation, and in extreme cases, **the death penalty**. The law allows for rehabilitation instead of prison for first-time low-level users, but trafficking remains punishable by the harshest penalties described above.

Thus, while the UAE has adopted slightly more lenient measures for minor, personal drug offenses, especially for tourists, the possession or consumption of cannabis—even in medicinal form—and any form of synthetic cannabinoids or hard drugs remains illegal. Those found in breach, even accidentally, risk severe legal repercussions. **Visitors should under no circumstances carry or use any drug-related substance in the UAE.**

In the UAE, drug offenses are governed by **federal law**, with **no distinctions** between public and private settings—possession, use, or importation of illegal drugs is strictly prohibited **anywhere**, regardless of location.

Federal Law No. 14 of 1995 (amended by Decree 30/2021) states that even trace amounts of narcotics found in blood, urine, clothing, or personal items—whether at home or in public—constitute possession and carry legal consequences.[6] Consequently, using cannabis in a private residence is treated the same as doing so in a public place; penalties apply equally. Public consumption is not treated with special leniency nor stricter severity—it's fully criminalized the same way private use is. Meanwhile, **importing small amounts of THC-infused items** (for example, food or drinks) is now sometimes penalized with **only confiscation or fines**, depending on whether it's a first offense, but personal consumption within the UAE is still illegal regardless of venue.

6 https://www.lexismiddleeast.com/law/UnitedArabEmirates/DecreeLaw_30_2021

Prescription Medication

Travelers to the UAE must follow strict regulations when bringing prescription and over-the-counter medications. The UAE classifies medications into categories such as **controlled substances**, which include narcotics, psychotropics, and certain stimulants like those used to treat ADHD. These drugs require **prior approval from the UAE Ministry of Health and Prevention (MOHAP)**. Visitors may bring up to a three-month supply, while residents can carry up to a twelve-month supply, but only if they have a MOHAP-issued electronic permit.

To obtain this permit, travelers must **apply online**, typically using UAE PASS, and submit documents such as a recent prescription (written within the last three months), a valid medical report (within one year), and a copy of their passport or Emirates ID. These medications must be in their original packaging and declared at customs upon arrival. Failing to follow these procedures can lead to **serious legal repercussions**, including confiscation, fines as high as 100,000–200,000 AED (approximately $27,200–$54,400 USD), imprisonment, deportation, and travel bans—even for small, undeclared quantities.[7]

For prescription medications that are **not classified as controlled, no prior approval is needed.** However, travelers are still limited to a three-month supply and must carry a valid prescription along with the medication in its original packaging. While over-the-counter (OTC) medications like ibuprofen or paracetamol are generally permitted, it is strongly recommended to carry a doctor's note to avoid issues, especially if the medication contains substances such as pseudoephedrine or codeine, which are controlled in the UAE. Even small amounts of restricted OTC medications have led to arrests in the past.

As of June 2025, new customs regulations require that **only approved medications may be carried in cabin baggage.** Other medications must be packed in checked luggage or risk being confiscated. Travelers are advised to consult MOHAP's approved medication list before flying and

7 https://mohap.gov.ae/en/w/issue-of-permit-to-import-medicines-for-personal-use

to declare all medications upon entry to the UAE. Full compliance with these laws ensures a safe and trouble-free visit, while any oversight could result in harsh legal consequences.

General Questions

1. ***Is cannabis legal in the UAE?*** **No.** Cannabis is unequivocally **illegal** in the UAE for any purpose—medical or recreational. Even trace amounts detected in your system, on personal items, or in transit can lead to criminal charges. Federal law imposes a **minimum three-month prison sentence** and fines (with penalties increasing on subsequent offenses.

2. ***Is there any place where I can legally purchase marijuana in the UAE?*** **No.** There are **no legal outlets whatsoever** for cannabis—whether recreational or medical—in the UAE. You **cannot purchase marijuana legally** at dispensaries, pharmacies, clinics, or online. Any attempt to obtain cannabis is illegal and subject to severe penalties under UAE law.

3. ***Can I have marijuana on my person or in hotel room in the UAE?*** **No.** You cannot have marijuana on your person or even in the privacy of your hotel room in the UAE. Possession is illegal and can lead to severe penalties.

4. ***Are there any other exceptions to the possession and consumption of cannabis in the UAE?*** **No.** There are **no exceptions** to the possession and consumption of cannabis in the UAE. All forms of cannabis are strictly illegal, with no allowances or exemptions.

5. ***What are the penalties for possessing and consuming other types of illicit drugs in the UAE?*** In the UAE, possession and consumption of any illicit drugs carry severe penalties. For first-time offenders, the punishment can include at least three months

in prison and fines between 20,000 and 100,000 AED (about $5,445 to $27,225 USD). Repeat offenders face a minimum of six months in prison and similar fines, while third-time offenders can receive at least two years in jail and fines starting at 100,000 AED (about $27,225 USD). Foreign nationals may also be deported. The UAE enforces a strict zero-tolerance policy on all illicit drugs, and even small amounts can lead to prosecution.

Law of the Land True Story [8]

Maurice Kevin O'Rourke, a 64-year-old Canadian from Mississauga, is facing a life sentence in a Dubai prison after authorities discovered over 100 grams of cannabis products in his luggage during a layover in July 2024. His wife, Pamela O'Rourke, says the cannabis and CBD oil were used to treat his chronic pain from Addison's disease, though they were not prescribed.

Despite his medical condition and age, UAE authorities are enforcing their strict zero-tolerance drug laws. Since his arrest, O'Rourke has undergone two surgeries and reportedly has not had access to his regular medications. His family is pleading for compassion, and his legal team plans to appeal the sentence on December 25.

The Canadian government has acknowledged his detention but has not commented further. Advocacy group *Detained in Dubai* is urging diplomatic action, citing past successful interventions. The case highlights the risks tourists face when traveling with cannabis—even for medical use—to countries with harsh drug laws like the UAE.

8 https://www.cbc.ca/news/canada/toronto/detained-in-dubai-cannabis-1.7410324

Takeaways

- The UAE enforces some of the strictest drug laws globally, applying **zero tolerance** to cannabis, synthetic cannabinoids, and all illicit narcotics. Even trace amounts can lead to imprisonment or heavy fines, whether detected in blood tests or on personal items.
- Recent legal reforms have slightly eased consequences for first-time possession of small amounts of cannabis or THC-infused products, often resulting in confiscation rather than imprisonment. However, all cannabis use, including medicinal forms like CBD oil, remains illegal and punishable by jail time and fines.
- Possession or trafficking of "classic" hard drugs such as cocaine, heroin, LSD, and methamphetamines carries harsh penalties, including minimum four-year prison sentences, large fines, deportation, and in extreme cases, the death penalty.
- Prescription medications, especially controlled substances, require prior approval and permits from UAE health authorities. Failure to declare or comply with medication import rules can result hefty fines imprisonment, and deportation.
- The UAE criminalizes drug possession and use equally in both private and public settings. There are no exceptions or allowances for cannabis or any illicit drugs, and even small quantities or trace amounts can result in severe legal consequences.

CHAPTER 5

ALCOHOL-RELATED OFFENSES

IN THIS CHAPTER

- Alcohol-Related Offenses
- Alcohol Regulation
- Things to Remember
- General Questions
- Law of the Land Hypothetical
- Takeaways

CHAPTER 5
ALCOHOL-RELATED OFFENSES

Alcohol-Related Offenses

The United Arab Emirates has long maintained a complex relationship with alcohol, shaped by its Islamic heritage and rapid modernization. Traditionally, alcohol is considered ***haram*—forbidden—under Islamic law**, and for many Emiratis, abstaining from alcohol remains a core religious and cultural value. As a result, alcohol historically had no place in everyday Emirati life, and until recently, strict laws criminalized its possession, consumption, or purchase without special permits.

Despite this, **alcohol is partially legal and available in the UAE with important restrictions**. Over the past few years, particularly in cosmopolitan cities like **Dubai** and **Abu Dhabi**, the laws have relaxed to accommodate the country's growing expatriate population and its ambitions as a global tourism destination. Alcohol can now be purchased without a special license in Dubai by non-Muslim residents and tourists, provided it is bought from licensed stores or consumed in licensed venues such as hotels, bars, and restaurants. Tourists can also buy alcohol upon arrival at duty-free shops. In contrast, **other emirates completely prohibit the sale and consumption of alcohol, and violations there carry more severe penalties**. For Muslim residents throughout the UAE, the purchase or consumption of alcohol remains illegal regardless of location or circumstances.

As legal reforms continue, the country walks a careful line between maintaining its religious identity and embracing international norms. Travelers are strongly advised to respect these laws and to consume alcohol only in permitted locations.

Alcohol Regulation[9]

Alcohol consumption in the United Arab Emirates is governed by a combination of federal and emirate-specific laws, rooted in Islamic principles but adapted to accommodate the country's large expatriate and tourist population. Regulations vary by emirate, but as mentioned above, however even where allowed, **only non-Muslims over the age of 21 consume alcohol—and only in licensed establishments or private spaces.**

For example, Dubai and Abu Dhabi allow alcohol for non-Muslims who are at least 21 years old. Tourists and residents no longer need a liquor license to buy or drink alcohol in licensed venues, however licensed retailers and establishments—such as bars, clubs, restaurants, and hotels—are the only places alcohol can be legally purchased and consumed. Drinking in public places or being visibly intoxicated in public remains a criminal offense. Likewise, driving under the influence of alcohol is strictly prohibited, with a **zero-tolerance policy**: even minimal blood alcohol content can lead to arrest, fines, license suspension, jail time, or deportation.

On the other hand, the **Emirate of Sharjah prohibits alcohol entirely**. In Sharjah, any possession or consumption of alcohol is a criminal offense, and penalties can include **imprisonment and heavy fines**. Enforcement across the UAE includes police patrols, surveillance in public areas, and strict border and customs controls. Individuals found violating alcohol laws—such as drinking without a license (in emirates where it's required), public intoxication, or alcohol possession in a dry emirate—can face **imprisonment**, **fines** ranging from 1,000 AED to

9 https://www.worldnomads.com/travel-safety/middle-east/united-arab-emirates/drinking-and-the-united-arab-emirates-dont-mix

20,000 AED (approximately $270 to $5,450 USD), or **deportation for foreign nationals.**

Things to Remember

- **Drinking Age:** The legal drinking age across most of the UAE is **21 years old** (and must be non-Muslim). Serving or selling alcohol to anyone under this age is a criminal offense.
- **ID: Valid photo ID** (such as a passport or Emirates ID) is required to purchase alcohol at licensed venues and retailers. Establishments are obligated to check ID to ensure buyers are of legal drinking age and non-Muslim.
- **Public consumption:** Drinking alcohol in public spaces or carrying open containers in the street is **illegal.** Alcohol may only be consumed in private residences or licensed establishments like hotels, bars, and clubs.
- **Public drunkenness:** Being drunk in public is a **criminal offense.** Penalties include arrest, fines, jail time, and possible deportation. Even slight intoxication in public can result in legal consequences.
- **Drunk Driving:** The UAE has a **zero-tolerance policy for drunk driving.** The legal blood alcohol limit is **0.0%.** Penalties include heavy fines (up to 20,000 AED or approximately $5,450 USD), **license suspension, imprisonment,** and **possible deportation** for expats or tourists.
- **Purchase of alcohol:** Alcohol can only be purchased from **licensed shops and venues** in emirates like Dubai and Abu Dhabi. These include hotel bars, restaurants, and duty-free airport stores. Tourists now only need a passport and **proof of being non-Muslim** in most emirates.
- **Alcohol Permits:** For private parties in licensed venues (such as hotels or clubs), no additional permit is usually required. However, **serving alcohol at private events in residential spaces may require a liquor license for residents,** depending on the

emirate. Large public events may require **special permits** from local authorities.

- **Illegal Alcohol:** Illegal alcohol (bootleg or homemade) is a significant issue in some areas. Consuming or possessing unlicensed or counterfeit alcohol can result in **serious health risks and criminal penalties**, including imprisonment and deportation.

General Questions

1. ***Can I possess an open container in public?*** **No.** You **cannot possess an open container of alcohol in public** in the UAE. It is illegal to carry or consume alcohol in public places such as streets, beaches, parks, or vehicles, even if you are of legal drinking age. Violating this law can result in fines, arrest, jail time, and possible deportation, especially if you are found to be intoxicated.

2. ***Can I drink in my hotel room?*** **Yes.** You can legally drink alcohol in your hotel room in the UAE, as **long as the hotel is licensed to serve alcohol.** Most international hotels in cities like Dubai and Abu Dhabi have alcohol licenses, and guests are permitted to consume alcohol in their private rooms. However, you must be of **legal drinking age (21 years or older)** and should not cause any disturbances or public intoxication, even within the hotel premises. Always drink responsibly, as rowdy behavior or intoxication in public areas of the hotel can still lead to legal trouble.

Law of the Land Hypothetical

HYPOTHETICAL: *James, a 30-year-old tourist from Australia, visits Dubai with a group of friends. One evening, they enjoy drinks at a licensed hotel bar. After a few cocktails, James decides to walk back to his hotel—just a few blocks away. On the way, he stumbles and gets into a verbal disagreement with another pedestrian. Police are called, and officers suspect James is intoxicated in public. Can James be arrested for public intoxication in the UAE even though he legally drank at a licensed venue?*

ANSWER: *Yes. James can be arrested. In the UAE, being drunk in public is a criminal offense, regardless of whether the alcohol was consumed legally. Even though James drank at a licensed establishment, once he stepped outside intoxicated, he became subject to strict public decency and conduct laws. He could face fines, temporary detention, or even deportation depending on the severity of his behavior and the judgment of local authorities.*

Takeaways

- You can legally drink alcohol in the UAE if you are at least 21 years old, but only in licensed venues such as certain hotels, bars, and private clubs. Public consumption is strictly prohibited.
- Possessing an open container or drinking alcohol in public places, including streets and beaches, is illegal and can result in arrest, fines, or even jail time.
- While Dubai and Abu Dhabi have relaxed rules around purchasing alcohol, in the past non-Muslim residents needed a permit. Now, tourists and residents can buy alcohol from licensed retailers without a permit in most emirates.
- The UAE has a **zero-tolerance policy** for drinking and driving. Any trace of alcohol in your system while operating a vehicle can lead to arrest, heavy fines, imprisonment, and deportation.

- Tourists may legally drink in their hotel rooms if the hotel is licensed. However, intoxicated behavior outside private spaces—such as hallways, lobbies, or streets—can still result in prosecution.

CHAPTER 6

FIREARM & AMMUNITION OFFENSES

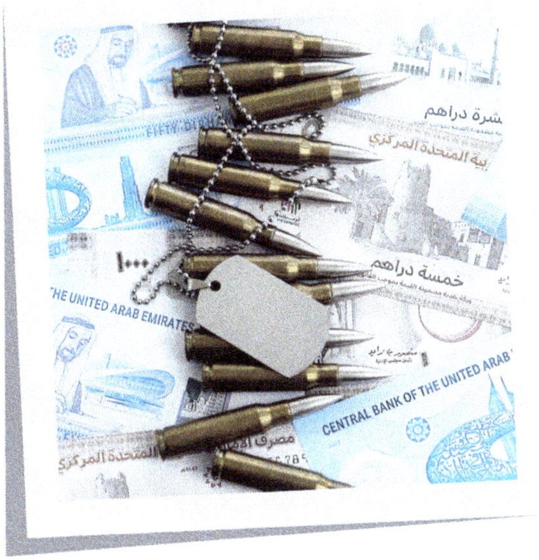

IN THIS CHAPTER

- Current Firearm Status and Related Penalties
- Firearm Restrictions for Visitors
- General Questions
- Law of the Land Hypothetical
- Takeaways

CHAPTER 6

FIREARM & AMMUNITION OFFENSES

Current Firearm Status and Related Penalties

Non-Muslim residents and visitors generally **cannot legally own firearms** in the UAE. Legally purchasing a gun is reserved almost exclusively for **UAE citizens**, and in some cases, **Gulf Cooperation Council (GCC) nationals or diplomats** with special permits. Civilians granted a license may own up to **three firearms**, such as hunting rifles, shotguns, pistols (up to 9 mm), bolt-action rifles, and air guns. Full automatics are prohibited.

To obtain a license, applicants must meet strict criteria: be a UAE citizen (or GCC national), at least **21 years old**, pass criminal and mental health checks, complete firearm proficiency training at approved shooting clubs, justify ownership (e.g., hunting, sport shooting, home defense), and secure proper home storage. Expats may only qualify by obtaining a home country no-objection certificate along with UAE Ministry approval, which is very uncommon.

Carrying a firearm in public requires a separate **concealed carry permit** beyond home ownership. Authorized firearms must be kept **concealed**, **unloaded**, and **off-limits** in military, government, or sensitive areas.

Licensed individuals may shoot only at approved ranges or on legal hunting trips. Use of a gun in **self-defense** is **permitted inside private property only**. Discharging weapons elsewhere or using them unlawfully carries severe penalties.

Penalties[10]

The United Arab Emirates enforces extremely strict penalties related to firearms. Possession of illegal firearms is a serious criminal offense and can result in imprisonment and fines. The severity of the penalty depends on the type of firearm and whether it is classified as automatic, military-grade, or otherwise prohibited. Individuals found in possession of such weapons may face minimum three years in prison, and in more severe cases, longer terms. If the weapon is linked to any criminal act or extremist motive, the sentence can be significantly harsher.

Trafficking and smuggling firearms across UAE borders is treated as a major threat to national security. This offense may result in life imprisonment or even the death penalty, particularly if the weapons are tied to organized crime or terrorism. The law applies equally to nationals, residents, and visitors, with no leniency shown in cases involving the illegal movement of arms into or out of the country.

Using a firearm during the commission of a crime greatly escalates the legal consequences. Whether the weapon is fired or simply brandished, its involvement in violent acts such as robbery, assault, or threats can lead to life imprisonment. If someone is killed as a result, the perpetrator may face the death penalty. Even without injury, the use of firearms in crimes is viewed with zero tolerance by the UAE legal system.

Carrying a firearm without proper authorization or in unauthorized public settings is also criminalized. Even licensed gun owners are

10 https://alshaibaadvocates.ae/understanding-the-uae-weapon-laws/

required to follow highly specific rules regarding transportation and storage. Carrying a weapon outside permitted zones or without valid documentation can result in imprisonment and the permanent revocation of any firearm license. The UAE does not recognize any right to bear arms in public, and carrying weapons outside of designated private or sporting settings is illegal.

Involvement in organized crime, particularly when it includes the possession, trafficking, or use of firearms, is treated with utmost severity. UAE anti-terror and anti-organized crime laws treat firearm-related offenses within criminal networks as an extreme danger to public safety. Those convicted may face long-term imprisonment or capital punishment. These laws reflect the UAE's broader zero-tolerance approach to weapons and their use, designed to preserve domestic security and public order.

Firearm Restrictions for Visitors

Non-citizens—whether **residents**, **tourists**, or **business travelers**—are **generally not allowed** to bring firearms into the country or possess them while there. The UAE does not permit visitors to carry or own firearms under any normal circumstances, and doing so without prior explicit authorization is considered a serious criminal offense.

Visitors are not allowed to import firearms, ammunition, or any weapon-like items into the UAE, even if they are licensed to own them in their home country. Possession of such items without official permission can result in **arrest at the border**, **confiscation of the items**, **heavy fines**, **imprisonment**, and even **deportation**. Firearm ownership is restricted almost entirely to UAE citizens, and even for them, it is tightly controlled under the supervision of the Ministry of Interior.

There are **no exceptions** for foreign tourists traveling for recreational purposes, including hunting or sport shooting, unless they are invited as part of an officially sanctioned event and granted temporary firearm licenses through official diplomatic channels and proper UAE authorities in advance. These are rare and must be approved before arrival in the country.

Carrying or transporting firearms, even replicas or antique weapons, without government authorization is strictly prohibited. Visitors caught with firearms face prosecution under the UAE's federal arms and ammunition laws, which impose strict sentences, including imprisonment for several years. The country takes a zero-tolerance approach to weapons possession due to national security concerns, and enforcement is aggressive at all entry points including airports, seaports, and land borders.

For tourists, business travelers, and other foreign nationals visiting the UAE, the best and safest course of action is to **avoid carrying any type of weapon or related item entirely**. This includes not only firearms but also items like stun guns, tasers, knives exceeding legal blade limits, and tactical gear. The consequences for non-compliance are severe and could have long-term legal and diplomatic repercussions.

General Questions

1. ***What happens if the police catch me carrying a firearm in the UAE?*** If police catch you carrying a firearm in the UAE without proper authorization, you can face severe legal consequences. Penalties typically include immediate arrest, confiscation of the weapon, criminal prosecution, and potentially a prison sentence ranging from several years to life, depending on the circumstances and type of firearm. If you're a non-citizen, deportation and a permanent ban from returning to the UAE are also likely outcomes after serving a sentence. The UAE enforces a zero-tolerance policy on illegal weapons possession, and even claiming ignorance of the law is not considered a valid defense.

2. ***What is the potential sentence for a firearms violation upon conviction?*** A conviction for a firearms violation in the UAE

can result in extremely harsh penalties, reflecting the country's strict stance on weapons control. The sentence depends on the nature of the offense, but for illegal possession, smuggling, or unauthorized use of firearms, prison terms typically range from 3 years to life imprisonment, along with substantial fines. If the firearm was used in the commission of a crime, the sentence can escalate to life in prison or even the death penalty, particularly if the act resulted in loss of life. Non-citizens convicted of firearms offenses are usually deported after serving their sentence, with a permanent ban on re-entry into the UAE.

Law of the Land Hypothetical

HYPOTHETICAL: *Sarah, a tourist from Canada, arrives in Dubai for a two-week vacation. Unaware of UAE regulations, she carries a small pocket pistol legally licensed in her home country, tucked in her luggage. At the airport customs inspection, officials discover the firearm. Sarah did not declare it or obtain any UAE authorization prior to travel. What are the legal consequences Sarah faces for attempting to bring a firearm into the UAE as a tourist without authorization?*

ANSWER: *In the UAE, non-citizens—including tourists—are prohibited from bringing firearms or ammunition into the country without explicit prior approval from the government. This restriction applies regardless of whether the firearm is legally licensed in the traveler's home country. By attempting to bring the unauthorized firearm into the UAE, Sarah violated federal arms laws. As a result, the firearm was immediately confiscated, and Sarah was arrested with criminal charges for illegal importation and possession of a firearm. The legal consequences she could face include imprisonment for several years, heavy fines, deportation after serving any sentence, and a permanent ban from returning to the UAE. Ignorance of the law is not accepted, and failure to comply with these rules leads to severe penalties and lasting legal difficulties.*

Takeaways

- Firearm ownership is tightly restricted and generally limited to UAE citizens with special licenses. Visitors and residents who are not citizens are prohibited from owning or carrying firearms under almost all circumstances.
- The penalties for firearms violations are severe, including long prison terms, heavy fines, deportation for foreigners, and even the death penalty if a firearm is used in a violent crime.
- Possession without authorization is treated as a serious criminal offense, regardless of intent or whether the weapon was loaded or used. This includes carrying, transporting, or storing firearms illegally.
- The UAE enforces a zero-tolerance policy on weapons trafficking, smuggling, and organized criminal involvement with firearms. Law enforcement agencies maintain high levels of surveillance, and courts apply strict sentencing guidelines to maintain public safety.

CHAPTER 7

PROSTITUTION

IN THIS CHAPTER

- Overview
- Laws and Penalties
- Prostitution Practices
- Sex Trafficking and Exploitation
- Sex Tourism and Public Health
- Law of the Land True Story
- Takeaways

CHAPTER 7

PROSTITUTION

Overview

Prostitution is **strictly illegal** in the United Arab Emirates. Engaging in, promoting, or facilitating prostitution is considered a criminal offense under UAE law, with penalties including imprisonment, fines, and deportation for foreign nationals. Authorities also target related offenses like operating or managing brothels and human trafficking.

Despite its illegality, prostitution persists in underground networks, often linked to human trafficking. Many individuals involved are migrant women lured with promises of legitimate jobs, only to be exploited. Key drivers include poverty, lack of employment opportunities in home countries, and the demand created by a large, transient male workforce, particularly in cities like Dubai and Abu Dhabi.

The UAE has a conservative society rooted in Islamic values, which strongly condemns prostitution as immoral and illegal. Public discussion of the issue is limited, and the government enforces strict moral codes. However, there is growing recognition of the need to address the issue through anti-trafficking laws and victim support rather than solely punitive measures.

Laws and Penalties

Prostitution in the UAE carries serious legal consequences. Under **Federal Law No. 3 of 1987**, often referred to as the UAE Penal Code, prostitution and all related activities—such as **solicitation**, **brothel-keeping**, and **pimping**—are **considered criminal offenses**. There is no legal framework that allows or regulates sex work in the country, and all such acts are viewed as violations of public morality and Islamic values.

Unlike some countries where prostitution is managed through red-light districts or government oversight, the UAE does not have any designated areas for such activities. Although prostitution does exist underground in certain nightlife areas, particularly in large cities like Dubai and Abu Dhabi, these activities are not sanctioned or regulated in any way. Law enforcement authorities actively monitor areas known for potential illicit activity, including some hotels, clubs, and massage parlors, and conduct regular raids to combat such offenses.

Because prostitution is illegal, there are no formal requirements or protections for individuals involved in sex work. Foreign nationals, who make up the majority of those arrested for prostitution, often come to the UAE under false pretenses and are later coerced or trafficked into the sex trade. When caught, they face legal proceedings that typically result in **imprisonment, fines, and mandatory deportation**.

Penalties for prostitution-related offenses vary depending on the nature of the crime. Individuals found guilty of engaging in prostitution can receive prison sentences ranging from one to three years. More severe punishment is applied to those involved in organizing or profiting from prostitution—such as traffickers and brothel operators—who may face up to 15 years in prison under **Federal Law No. 51 of 2006**, which focuses on human trafficking.[11] These measures reflect the UAE's strict legal stance against prostitution and its efforts to uphold conservative social values.

11 https://www4.aucegypt.edu/CMRS/Files/English.pdf

Prostitution Practices

Not only is prostitution in the UAE illegal, but it is also **deeply stigmatized.** Yet it persists in underground forms despite significant government enforcement. While exact figures are difficult to confirm due to the hidden nature of the activity, authorities reportedly arrest and deport between 5,000 to 6,000 individuals each year for prostitution-related offenses. In Dubai alone, over 1,700 arrests were made in 2023. These statistics suggest a **persistent problem**, with unofficial estimates indicating that as many as 30,000 individuals—primarily foreign women—may be involved in prostitution nationwide at any given time.[12]

Prostitution in the UAE takes various **covert forms**. Street prostitution is rare due to strict policing, but **massage parlors** have become a common front for illicit activity. Many of these so-called "spas" offer sexual services in back rooms, despite frequent police raids. **Escort services**, often advertised online or arranged through messaging apps like WhatsApp and Telegram, are another widespread method. Some cases involve organized brothels or **informal setups operating out of private apartments** or hotel rooms. These operations typically function through discreet networks and word-of-mouth, making detection difficult. Even so, authorities conduct regular stings and surveillance targeting such venues.

While the UAE maintains a firm legal and moral opposition to prostitution, its underground presence continues, fueled by organized networks and economic vulnerability. The government's efforts to crack down on such practices are extensive but face ongoing challenges, particularly in distinguishing between perpetrators and victims within a system that prioritizes punishment over protection.

12 https://en.wikipedia.org/wiki/Prostitution_in_the_United_Arab_Emirates?

Sex Trafficking and Exploitation

Sex trafficking and sexual exploitation are **serious and persistent concerns** in the United Arab Emirates, driven by a **combination of economic vulnerability, demand for illicit services**, and the **country's role as a global transit and labor destination.** Although the UAE has strict laws prohibiting all forms of human trafficking, including sex trafficking, the issue continues largely underground and affects a significant number of foreign women.

The UAE functions primarily as a **destination country for trafficking victims.** Women from countries such as Uganda, Kenya, the Philippines, Morocco, Ethiopia, and parts of Eastern Europe are often recruited with false promises of legitimate employment in sectors like domestic work, hospitality, or retail. Upon arrival, many are coerced into prostitution through threats, debt bondage, document confiscation, and physical abuse. Some arrive legally on tourist or short-term work visas, only to be exploited after their entry. Traffickers frequently take advantage of visa loopholes, rotating or hiding victims to avoid detection.

Urban centers like **Dubai** and **Abu Dhabi** are particularly vulnerable to trafficking due to their large expatriate populations, tourism industries, and numerous entertainment venues. Although there are no officially designated red-light districts, certain hotels, massage parlors, and private residences have become informal hotspots for illicit sexual activity. These cities offer traffickers access to transient clients and cover for underground operations, making law enforcement efforts more challenging.

The demographic most at risk includes young, low-income migrant women—especially those traveling alone or recruited through unregulated or deceptive labor agencies. These women often lack legal support or knowledge of their rights, making them easy targets for exploitation. Cultural and legal barriers also discourage many victims from coming forward, especially when they fear prosecution for immigration or prostitution offenses.

The UAE government has taken significant steps to combat trafficking. Federal Law No. 51 of 2006, amended in 2023, imposes severe penalties—including life imprisonment—for human trafficking offenses. Specialized police units have been created to investigate trafficking cases, and the government has launched **public hotlines** and **victim shelters**. Facilities like the **Ewa'a Shelters for Women and Children** in Abu Dhabi and the **Dubai Foundation for Women and Children** provide medical care, legal aid, housing, and psychological counseling to survivors. The UAE also collaborates with international organizations such as the United Nations Office on Drugs and Crime (UNODC) and Interpol, and has participated in global training and capacity-building efforts aimed at identifying and protecting victims.

Despite these efforts, international watchdogs, including the U.S. Department of State, have pointed out several shortcomings in the UAE's approach. One of the most critical concerns is the **lack of effective victim identification**. Many trafficking victims continue to be detained, fined, or deported for violations such as prostitution or visa overstays without being properly screened or offered protection. Advocacy groups have called for more transparent investigations, better training for front-line officers, and stronger victim-centered policies.

Sex Tourism and Public Health

Dubai is the most commonly cited destination for sex tourism within the UAE. In the past, clubs like the infamous Cyclone in Dubai openly catered to foreign sex workers and tourists seeking illicit services before being shut down. Today, sex tourism is far more concealed, with massage parlors, nightclubs, and luxury hotels often acting as fronts for prostitution. These venues may employ women under other titles, such as "hostesses" or "spa therapists," but offer sexual services in back rooms or through private arrangements. Some escort services are organized online or through encrypted messaging apps like WhatsApp and Telegram. Rather than openly advertising services, these operations depend on word-of-mouth, social media groups, and personal referrals to avoid detection.

Public health concerns related to this underground sex trade are significant but difficult to measure due to the criminalized and hidden nature of the activity. Because sex work is illegal, there is no regulatory framework for health screening, condom use, or medical care for sex workers. This increases the risk of **sexually transmitted infections** (**STIs**), including HIV/AIDS, not only among sex workers but also among their clients and the broader public. Many sex workers lack access to regular medical services, and fear of arrest or deportation discourages them from seeking treatment. Additionally, the clandestine conditions under which they operate make it challenging for public health authorities to conduct outreach, distribute protective supplies, or collect accurate data.

Despite these risks, the UAE has not implemented harm-reduction programs specifically targeting sex workers or sex tourism. Instead, its public health policies emphasize prevention through strict law enforcement and deportation of individuals engaged in prostitution. As a result, public health concerns associated with sex tourism are often underreported and inadequately addressed in national health planning.

Law of the Land True Story[13]

In Dubai, behind the city's glittering skyline and luxury lifestyle, a far darker reality unfolds for many African women lured there with promises of opportunity. One of them, a Nigerian woman in her 20s, thought she was heading to a better life. Instead, she was taken to a parking lot in Ajman and forced to have sex with strangers while cars were being painted nearby. She was given nothing in return—not even

13 https://www.icij.org/investigations/trafficking-inc/how-torture-deception-and-inaction-underpin-the-uaes-thriving-sex-trafficking-industry/

money for food. When she tried to escape, she slept on the streets and begged until a Nigerian nurse helped her find a way home.

She's just one of many women deceived and brutalized by traffickers operating in the United Arab Emirates. Some, like Christy Gold—a woman who fled charges in Nigeria—present a glamorous image on social media while running criminal networks that coerce women into prostitution. Several victims say they were beaten, starved, and even tortured with chili paste as punishment for disobedience or not earning enough. They were warned they'd be dumped in the desert if they tried to escape.

These women were trapped not just by force but by deep psychological manipulation, spiritual threats, and crushing debts—sometimes as high as $15,000 USD. While the UAE has anti-trafficking laws on paper, many survivors and activists say authorities rarely help. Victims are often treated as criminals, detained for immigration or prostitution charges, and left with no support. Nigerian officials say requests for cooperation go unanswered. Human rights groups argue that the UAE turns a blind eye to the problem—allowing the sex trade to thrive in plain sight in clubs, backstreets, and even desert brothels. Behind the wealth and progress, these stories remind us that human trafficking is not just a crime—it's a crisis of suffering, silence, and survival.

Takeaways

- Prostitution is illegal and strictly punished in the UAE, with no legal framework for sex work. Offenses such as solicitation, brothel-keeping, and pimping can lead to imprisonment, fines, and deportation, especially for foreign nationals who make up the majority of those arrested.
- Despite strong legal and cultural opposition, prostitution persists in underground forms, including massage parlors, escort services, and informal brothels, particularly in urban centers like Dubai and Abu Dhabi. These activities are often connected to organized criminal networks and remain difficult for authorities to fully eradicate.

- Sex trafficking is a serious problem in the UAE, where vulnerable women from Africa, Asia, and Eastern Europe are lured under false pretenses and coerced into the sex trade. While the government has taken steps to address trafficking—including strict laws, shelters, and cooperation with international organizations—victim identification and protection remain weak points.
- Sex tourism exists unofficially in certain parts of the UAE, especially Dubai, where it operates through discreet channels such as hotels, massage parlors, and online platforms. These practices raise public health concerns due to the lack of regulation and healthcare access for sex workers, increasing the risk of sexually transmitted infections.
- The UAE's approach emphasizes criminal enforcement over harm reduction, with limited public health outreach or victim-centered services. As a result, both exploitation and health risks persist in the shadows, underscoring the challenges of balancing legal enforcement with human rights and public health protections.

CHAPTER 8

LGBTQ

IN THIS CHAPTER

- Homophobia in the UAE
- LGBTQ Legislation
- LGBTQ Tourism and Safety Concerns
- General Questions
- Law of the Land True Story

CHAPTER 8

LGBTQ

Homophobia in the UAE

In the United Arab Emirates, LGBTQ+ individuals face systemic legal discrimination, intense social stigma, and a complete lack of protection or recognition under the law. **Homosexuality is illegal** under both the country's civil and Sharia-based legal systems. Penalties can include imprisonment, fines, forced deportation, and—in theory—capital punishment, though no documented cases of the death penalty for same-sex acts have been reported in recent history.[14] Historically, the UAE's government has tightly aligned with conservative Islamic principles, and public morality laws are used to suppress any non-normative gender or sexual expression. There has never been legal acknowledgment or protection for LGBTQ+ people in the country.

Culturally, homophobia is deeply embedded in Emirati society. Public opinion reflects **overwhelming disapproval of LGBTQ+ identities**, fueled by a strong adherence to traditional Islamic teachings that label same-sex relations as sinful. Social and familial honor plays a major role in reinforcing heteronormativity; LGBTQ+ Emiratis face rejection, surveillance, or even violence if they come out to their families.

14 https://www.hrw.org/world-report/2023/country-chapters/united-arab-emirates

Fear of social shame and legal consequences means most LGBTQ+ people live closeted lives, often enduring extreme psychological stress and isolation. The government blocks LGBTQ+ content online and bans displays of pride symbols, while schools and workplaces offer no anti-discrimination protections and actively enforce conformity. In daily life, homophobic attitudes manifest in both overt and subtle forms. LGBTQ+ individuals risk job termination, housing discrimination, or arrest for simply dressing in a gender-nonconforming way or expressing affection in public. Transgender people in particular are targeted under vague public decency or impersonation laws, and there have been reports of arbitrary detention and forced physical examinations.

There are no statistics available from UAE authorities regarding violence or discrimination against LGBTQ+ people, largely due to censorship and fear of retaliation. However, anecdotal evidence from activists and international watchdogs documents recurring abuse, harassment, and lack of legal recourse.[15] There are no known public figures or cultural icons within the UAE who openly advocate for LGBTQ+ rights, as doing so would violate national laws and could result in arrest or exile. Even international celebrities have occasionally faced backlash for perceived LGBTQ+ support during performances or campaigns in the UAE, illustrating the regime's zero-tolerance stance.

Legally, there has been **no progress toward LGBTQ+ rights in recent years.** In fact, reforms touted as modernization efforts—such as updates to family or alcohol laws—have deliberately excluded anything related to sexual orientation or gender identity. The government maintains an image of religious and moral purity, and its silence or denial regarding LGBTQ+ issues continues to fuel an atmosphere of fear and repression. In this context, LGBTQ+ lives are not just invisible; they are criminalized and erased.

15 https://www.hrw.org/news/2021/06/29/uae-deepening-repression-overrides-facade-tolerance

LGBTQ Legislation

Same-sex relationships in the United Arab Emirates are explicitly criminalized under both the federal penal code and Islamic Sharia law. Article 356 of the previous penal code, along with provisions in the updated 2021 legal reforms, continues to **prohibit "indecent acts" between people of the same sex.** These laws are vaguely worded but routinely interpreted to mean that consensual same-sex activity is illegal. Offenses can lead to punishments including **imprisonment for up to 14 years, deportation for foreigners, fines,** and in rare cases, **corporal punishment** under Sharia-based interpretations—though these are seldom documented due to the secrecy surrounding prosecutions.[16]

There are no laws in the UAE that recognize or protect LGBTQ+ rights in any capacity. **Same-sex marriage, civil unions, or any legal acknowledgment of partnerships are prohibited.** The legal system does not provide transgender people with avenues to change their gender markers, and gender non-conforming expression is often treated as a form of public indecency or deception. Far from being neutral, the country's legislation is structured to suppress LGBTQ+ visibility and identity. Laws reinforce a rigid definition of gender and sexuality, punishing deviations as threats to public morality.

Discrimination based on sexual orientation or gender identity is not only legal but in many cases institutionalized. **The country's labor laws, civil service regulations, and school policies do not include any provisions to protect LGBTQ+ individuals from bias or abuse.** Employers are not obligated to maintain inclusive policies, and there is no avenue for legal recourse if someone is harassed or fired because of their identity. In fact, coming forward with such a complaint could potentially expose a person to legal danger themselves. Foreign workers, who make up the vast majority of the population, are particularly vulnerable because their

16 https://www.state.gov/reports/2023-country-reports-on-human-rights-practices/united-arab-emirates/

residency status depends on their employment and employer, meaning LGBTQ+ migrants are often doubly at risk.[17]

Geographically, there are **no safe zones or LGBTQ+-friendly areas within the UAE.** Cities like Dubai or Abu Dhabi may appear cosmopolitan on the surface due to their international populations and nightlife scenes, but the outward appearance of tolerance masks rigid legal enforcement. The state operates with intense surveillance, and even private gatherings can be monitored or reported. What might seem like relatively liberal attitudes among some urban expatriate circles quickly evaporates in the face of police intervention or public exposure. Smaller emirates such as Sharjah or Ajman are known for stricter enforcement of moral codes, and LGBTQ+ individuals face even higher risks of being targeted.

Overall, the legislative framework in the UAE not only fails to protect LGBTQ+ people—it actively criminalizes their existence. Legal silence in some areas is not a sign of neutrality but a deliberate absence of protections. In this climate, visibility is dangerous, and safety depends on staying hidden.

LGBTQ Tourism and Safety Concerns

LGBTQ tourism in the United Arab Emirates remains virtually nonexistent in any official or openly recognized form. The country does not promote itself as an LGBTQ-friendly destination, and there are no legal protections or specific accommodations for LGBTQ travelers. Travel marketing from the UAE focuses instead on luxury, architecture, shopping, and family-friendly entertainment, with no mention of inclusivity regarding sexual orientation or gender identity. Major international travel advisories, including those from the U.S. and U.K. governments, caution LGBTQ travelers that consensual same-sex relations are criminalized in the UAE and can lead to arrest, detention, and deportation.

17 https://www.hrw.org/world-report/2023/country-chapters/united-arab-emirates

While cities like Dubai and Abu Dhabi may appear more cosmopolitan on the surface due to their large expatriate populations and global business presence, this should not be mistaken for legal or cultural tolerance. The laws apply uniformly across the entire country, and the apparent openness in some areas is more about image management than genuine inclusion. **Visitors should not assume that urban centers are safe havens for LGBTQ expression.** Smaller emirates such as Sharjah or Fujairah tend to enforce conservative norms even more stringently, with less tolerance for any perceived deviance from traditional values.

Public displays of affection—regardless of sexual orientation—are discouraged in the UAE and can lead to warnings, fines, or legal consequences. For same-sex couples, these consequences can be far more serious. Holding hands, hugging, or kissing in public may be interpreted not only as indecent but as an explicit violation of the penal code, especially if the individuals are suspected of being in a same-sex relationship. Even wearing clothing deemed gender non-conforming or sharing a hotel room without clear evidence of a familial or heterosexual relationship can trigger scrutiny.

There are significant safety concerns for LGBTQ visitors. Arrests have occurred based on behavior, appearance, or online activity, including social media posts. Because the laws criminalize same-sex relations and provide no protection against discrimination or harassment, travelers who identify as LGBTQ may be at risk from both the legal system and informal forms of policing by citizens or hotel staff. Embassies have limited ability to intervene in such cases due to the UAE's strict application of its laws.

In short, while the UAE remains a major luxury travel hub, it is not a safe destination for LGBTQ tourism. Legal risks, lack of protections, and deeply conservative social attitudes mean that LGBTQ individuals must weigh the dangers carefully. Discretion is not just advisable—it is essential for personal safety.

General Questions

1. ***Do any laws in UAE protect homosexual expressions and conduct?*** **No.** The United Arab Emirates does not have any laws that protect homosexual expressions or conduct. On the contrary, same-sex sexual activity is criminalized under both federal and Sharia-based legal codes. Laws prohibit "indecent acts," "morality violations," and "acts contrary to the principles of Islam," which are interpreted to include same-sex relations and public or private displays of LGBTQ+ identity or affection. There are no legal protections against discrimination based on sexual orientation or gender identity in employment, housing, or public services. Instead of protective laws, LGBTQ+ individuals may face arrest, prosecution, or deportation for behavior interpreted as promoting or expressing homosexuality.

2. ***What is the punishment for homosexual expressions and conduct?*** Homosexual expressions and conduct can lead to severe penalties and punishments may include imprisonment, deportation for non-citizens, fines, corporal punishment, and—in theory—capital punishment under Sharia for consensual same-sex acts, though there are no known recent executions for such offenses. Typically, individuals found guilty of same-sex conduct face **prison sentences ranging from one to ten years**, particularly under Articles 356 and 358 of the UAE Penal Code, which address acts of "indecency" and "outrage against modesty." In practice, punishments are often harsher for non-citizens, who are also subject to **immediate deportation** after serving their sentence.

   Expressions such as cross-dressing, posting LGBTQ+ content online, or engaging in public displays of affection can also result in arrest and charges related to **"public morality" or "cybercrime" laws**. For example, under the UAE's Cybercrime Law, promoting or publishing content perceived as supportive of homosexuality may lead to **fines of up to 1,000,000 AED** (**about $272,000 USD**) and imprisonment.

Law of the Land True Story[18]

Disney's decision to open a theme park in Abu Dhabi is a strategic move aimed at expanding its global footprint without major financial risk. Announced in May 2025, the park will be built on Yas Island through a partnership with Miral, an Emirati developer that will fund and operate the site while Disney provides branding and creative input. With Abu Dhabi positioned within a four-hour flight of one-third of the world's population, the location offers massive potential for tourism and revenue growth.

However, this expansion puts Disney in a difficult position regarding LGBTQ+ rights. The UAE criminalizes homosexuality, and same-sex relationships can result in imprisonment or deportation. Public displays of affection—even between heterosexual couples—are tightly controlled, and LGBTQ+ content is frequently censored. For instance, the animated film Lightyear was banned in the UAE for including a same-sex kiss.

To be allowed into such a market with strict moral codes, Disney has to be practical and adapt its approach. While the company promotes diversity and inclusion globally, it recognizes that showcasing LGBTQ+ characters or events in Abu Dhabi would likely lead to legal and cultural pushback, possibly even the park's closure. Instead, Disney is expected to maintain inclusive internal policies for its staff while tailoring the guest experience to respect local laws and customs. Pride events and openly gay representation will almost certainly be absent, reflecting a compromise between Disney's values and the realities of operating in the UAE.

This pragmatic approach raises questions about whether Disney is sacrificing its principles for access to a lucrative market. Critics argue such compromises reinforce discriminatory norms, while others see Disney's presence as a potential, if limited, step toward broader cultural engagement. Ultimately, Disney's Abu Dhabi park highlights the

18 https://www.washingtontimes.com/news/2025/may/8/pro-lgbtq-disney-plans-latest-resort-anti-gay-abu-dhabi/

difficult balance global companies face when navigating markets with deeply different cultural and legal standards.

CHAPTER 9

SEXUALLY MOTIVATED/ VIOLENT CRIMES

IN THIS CHAPTER

- Overview
- Related Legislation
- General Questions
- Law of the Land Hypothetical
- Takeaways

CHAPTER 9

SEXUALLY MOTIVATED/ VIOLENT CRIMES

Overview

Sexually motivated crimes in the United Arab Emirates (UAE) are a significant concern, although they are often **underreported because of legal, cultural, and social barriers.** Reliable statistics are hard to come by since many victims fear being prosecuted themselves or facing social stigma. For example, Dubai Police estimate that only about 10% of sexual crimes against women are actually reported. Surveys have also shown that over half of women in the UAE would hesitate to report a rape to the authorities due to fears of being charged with extramarital sex, which is illegal under UAE law.

Several social, cultural, and economic factors contribute to this situation. The UAE's legal system places a heavy burden of proof on the victim in sexual assault cases, and victims risk being accused of extramarital sex (*zina*) when they come forward. This legal risk discourages reporting and often leads to under-enforcement. Culturally, there are deeply rooted gender norms and a strong emphasis on family honor, which can result in victim-blaming and social ostracism of survivors, further silencing them. The groups most affected tend to be **migrant domestic workers**--from countries such as India, Sri Lanka, and the Philippines--who face both economic and social vulnerabilities, as well as young women drawn to the country's high-profile social scene. Urban centers like Dubai and Abu Dhabi tend to be hotspots for such crimes due to their status as global hubs and destinations for expatriates and tourists. However, detailed regional data within the UAE is limited, making it difficult to assess variations across different emirates.

In summary, sexually motivated crimes in the UAE are more prevalent than official reports suggest. Legal frameworks, social norms, and economic inequalities create barriers that prevent many victims from seeking help or justice. Addressing these issues will require changes in the legal system, greater cultural awareness, and improved protections and support for victims.

Related Legislation

In the United Arab Emirates, sexually motivated crimes are addressed under **Federal Decree Law No. 31 of 2021** (Penal Code), which replaced the previous Penal Code and is part of a wider reform effort.[19] The law outlines specific crimes and their associated penalties, though enforcement is shaped by both legal codes and cultural norms.

Sexual assault, rape, harassment, and related offenses are criminalized, and penalties are generally severe. **Rape** is classified as a serious offense: under Article 409, the punishment can include **life imprisonment**, and in cases involving a minor (under 18), a person with a disability, or use of a weapon, **the death penalty** may be applied. **Sexual harassment**—which includes persistent or unwelcome advances or remarks—is punishable under Article 413, with penalties ranging from **6 months to 2 years in prison**, along with potential fines. If the offender is in a position of authority over the victim—such as a supervisor, doctor, or family member—the penalty increases.

There are also laws that criminalize **indecent assault** (Article 410), **voyeurism**, and **distribution of explicit materials**. The UAE takes a conservative view on public morality, so acts that might be seen as minor in other jurisdictions—like kissing in public—can also be prosecuted under decency laws.

19 https://www.uaelegislation.gov.ae/en/legislations

Despite the strong legal wording, enforcement is complicated. Victims of sexual crimes often fear being prosecuted themselves, especially women, due to the **application of "zina" laws** (Article 411), which criminalize sexual relations outside of marriage. If a victim reports a rape but cannot prove it under the strict evidentiary standards—traditionally requiring confession or multiple eyewitnesses—they risk being charged with consensual extramarital sex. This risk is especially pronounced for migrant women, who may lack the social and legal resources to defend themselves.

Recent reforms have aimed to improve protections for victims. These include measures to ensure victim confidentiality, allow medical professionals to report sexual violence, and reduce the chance of a victim being prosecuted for related conduct. For example, under reforms passed in 2020–2021, **pregnancy outside marriage is no longer automatically criminalized**, which had previously been a barrier to rape victims seeking help.

Nonetheless, enforcement remains inconsistent, and the cultural environment often discourages reporting. Legal aid is limited, particularly for low-income or migrant women, and male guardianship norms can influence how cases are handled at the police and prosecutorial levels. While the law provides tools for protection, practical justice depends on local interpretation and the specific emirate where the case is handled.

General Questions

1. ***Do laws in the UAE related to sex crimes protect the victims equally?*** **No.** While UAE laws criminalize rape, sexual assault, and harassment, and recent reforms have added some protections for victims, in practice victims are not always protected equally. Women who report rape risk being charged with extramarital sex if they can't prove it, which deters many from coming forward. Migrant women, especially domestic workers, face the

greatest barriers due to isolation, fear of deportation, and lack of legal support. Cultural pressures and inconsistent enforcement also make justice harder to access. So while the laws exist, equal protection remains uneven.

2. ***Pursuant to law, what is the age of consent for sex in the UAE?*** **The UAE does not recognize an age of consent for sex.** All sexual activity outside marriage is illegal, regardless of age or consent. Only married heterosexual couples can legally have sex. If a minor is involved, it's treated as statutory rape, with severe penalties like life imprisonment or even death in aggravated cases.

Law of the Land Hypothetical

HYPOTHETICAL: *Emma, a 24-year-old British tourist, attends a private yacht party in Dubai. She meets a man and, after a few drinks, they engage in consensual sex at his hotel. The next morning, a dispute arises, and hotel staff report the incident. Police question both parties. Emma explains that the sex was consensual, but they are not married. Can Emma be prosecuted even if the sex was consensual and both parties are adults?*

ANSWER: *Yes. In the UAE, consensual sex outside of marriage is still a criminal offense under the Penal Code. Emma and the man could both be charged with "zina" (extramarital sex), regardless of consent or age. While recent reforms have reduced prosecution in some cases, especially if there's no pregnancy or complaint, enforcement can vary. Even as a tourist, Emma risks arrest, a jail sentence, and deportation depending on how authorities handle the case. Tourists and non-Muslims are subject to the same legal standards in the UAE regarding sex-related laws. The UAE's Penal Code applies to everyone, regardless of religion or nationality.*

Takeaways

Sexually motivated crimes are significantly underreported due to fear of prosecution, social stigma, and strict evidentiary requirements. Many victims—especially women—risk being charged with extramarital sex (zina) if they report assault and cannot meet legal proof standards.

The UAE Penal Code (Federal Decree Law No. 31 of 2021) criminalizes rape, harassment, and other sex-related offenses with severe penalties, including life imprisonment or death in aggravated cases. However, enforcement is inconsistent and shaped by local norms.

Legal reforms in 2020–2021 aimed to protect victims better—such as ending automatic prosecution for pregnancy outside marriage—but challenges remain, especially for low-income and migrant women with limited access to justice.

All sexual activity outside marriage is illegal in the UAE, and there is no legal age of consent. Even consensual sex between unmarried adults, including tourists and non-Muslims, can lead to arrest, imprisonment, or deportation.

Social, cultural, and economic factors—like male guardianship norms, gender expectations, and migrant labor vulnerabilities—create systemic barriers to justice, making the law unevenly applied and difficult for many victims to safely navigate.

CHAPTER 10

ARRESTED IN THE UAE

IN THIS CHAPTER

- Overview
- The Arrest Process
- Getting Legal Assistance
- Bail
- Complaints Against the Police
- General Questions

CHAPTER 10

ARRESTED IN THE UAE

Overview

When traveling in a foreign country, it's imperative to recognize that you are subject to the legal jurisdiction and regulations of that nation. These laws may significantly differ from those in your home country and might not offer the same legal protections you are accustomed to. It's crucial to bear in mind that penalties for violating foreign laws can be more severe than those for similar offenses in your home country, and ignorance of these laws is not typically accepted as a defense.

The consequences for breaking the law while abroad can be severe and may include expulsion, fines, arrest, or imprisonment. Even unintentional violations can lead to serious legal repercussions. It is essential for travelers to be aware of and adhere to the laws of the host country to avoid legal entanglements and ensure a safe and enjoyable experience.

Specifically, stringent penalties are often enforced for possession, use, or trafficking of illegal drugs in many countries. Convicted offenders can expect severe consequences, including lengthy jail sentences and hefty fines. The legal processes for foreigners in the event of an arrest abroad involve being charged or indicted, prosecuted, potentially convicted and sentenced, and, if applicable, going through an appeals process.

Navigating a foreign legal system can be complex, and individuals arrested abroad must be prepared to comply with the legal procedures of the host country. Seeking legal representation and understanding the local legal nuances are crucial steps for those facing legal issues in a foreign jurisdiction.

Awareness of and adherence to the laws of a foreign country are paramount when traveling. Understanding the potential consequences for legal violations and being prepared to navigate the legal system of the host country are essential aspects of responsible international travel.

The Arrest Process

In the UAE, you can be arrested for a wide range of offenses, many of which may seem minor or overlooked in other countries. Crimes include not only serious offenses like theft, assault, and drug possession, but also **morality-based violations** such as public displays of affection, drunkenness, unmarried cohabitation, sex outside marriage, homosexual conduct, and offensive social media posts. Even swearing in public or flipping someone off can lead to arrest under public decency or cybercrime laws.

The arrest process usually begins when the police receive a complaint or witness an incident. They may detain the person on the spot or summon them to a station for questioning. Unlike in many Western systems, **there is no guaranteed right to remain silent, and suspects may not immediately have access to a lawyer.** Detainees can be held for **up to 48 hours** before being presented to the public prosecution. The prosecution then decides whether to release, extend detention, or press formal charges. Detention can be extended while the case is under investigation.

For expats and tourists, the consequences can be more severe. Being unfamiliar with local laws, they may unknowingly break rules—such as drinking alcohol without a license or sharing a hotel room with someone of the opposite sex. In many cases, expats or tourists are **deported after serving a sentence**, or even without trial if the offense is considered damaging to public morals or national security. Visitors should also know that **bail is not always granted**, especially for serious offenses or if the accused is considered a flight risk. Language barriers, lack of local legal knowledge, and limited access to legal counsel can complicate the situation further.

In short, the UAE enforces strict laws with **a conservative moral code**, and the arrest process can be swift and intimidating. Expats and tourists should be especially cautious, as ignorance of the law is not a defense, and minor actions could result in serious legal trouble.

Getting Legal Assistance

In the United Arab Emirates, **the right to legal counsel is protected by law.** According to the UAE Criminal Procedure Code, anyone accused of a crime has the right to hire a lawyer to represent them during the investigation and trial process. While this right is guaranteed, it is important to understand that legal representation is **not automatically provided**; the accused **must request a lawyer,** and if they cannot afford one, the court may appoint a legal representative on their behalf. Lawyers must be licensed to practice in the UAE, especially in criminal cases.

Foreign nationals enjoy the same right to legal counsel as UAE citizens. It is crucial for foreign residents or visitors to notify authorities of their nationality so they can receive appropriate consular assistance. Foreigners can hire local lawyers, and in cases involving labor or immigration issues, special procedures may apply. When arrested, individuals should remain calm and request a lawyer immediately. **It is important to avoid signing any documents or making statements without legal representation present**. Also, individuals should inform authorities of their nationality and ask to contact their embassy or consulate. Communicating with family or trusted contacts as soon as possible is also recommended.

Embassies and consulates serve as important support systems for nationals facing legal trouble in the UAE. While they cannot intervene to free someone from detention or influence legal outcomes, they provide critical assistance such as visiting detainees, ensuring their wellbeing, offering lists of local lawyers who speak their language, and facilitating communication with family. Embassies also monitor cases to ensure fair treatment and proper legal procedures.

Regarding legal aid, the **UAE does not have a broad or centralized free legal aid system** like some Western countries. However, certain government bodies offer limited assistance. For example, the **Dubai Legal Affairs Department** provides some help for low-income individuals within Dubai, and the **Abu Dhabi Judicial Department** offers legal advice services that may sometimes be free or low cost. There are also a few NGOs and community organizations that can assist in finding affordable legal counsel, though these options are limited. Pro bono services are rare but occasionally available through private law firms. The UAE Ministry of Justice has initiatives aimed at improving legal access, but private legal representation is often necessary. Local attorneys can be found through your home embassy or consulate.

For example, the U.S. Embassy in the UAE provides a useful list of local lawyers and consular services at **https://ae.usembassy.gov/u-s-citizen-services/local-resources-of-u-s-citizens/lawyers/**.

If someone finds themselves in legal trouble in the UAE, it is vital to stay calm, request legal counsel without delay, inform the authorities of your nationality, and contact your embassy or consulate immediately to receive the best possible assistance.

Bail[20]

In the United Arab Emirates, a bail system does exist as part of the criminal justice process, but it operates somewhat differently from what many might expect in Western countries. Bail allows a person accused of a crime to be released from custody while awaiting trial, typically under certain conditions or after providing a financial guarantee. However,

20 https://aws-legalgroup.com/bail-granted

whether bail is granted depends heavily on the nature of the crime, the risk of flight, and the judge's discretion.

When bail is granted, it usually requires the accused or a guarantor to deposit a sum of money as a security to ensure the person will appear for their court dates. This amount can vary widely depending on the seriousness of the offense and other factors. Sometimes bail may come with restrictions, such as surrendering a passport or regular check-ins with authorities. It's important to understand that the judge may deny bail if they believe the accused poses a flight risk, or if the offense involves serious crimes like terrorism, drug trafficking, or violence.

Visitors to the UAE should be particularly cautious because **the bail system can be strict, and the amount set for bail might be high.** Foreign nationals may also face challenges such as difficulty providing guarantors or financial guarantees within the country. Additionally, bail conditions for visitors may include surrendering travel documents, which can delay or prevent travel until the case is resolved or bail conditions are lifted. For tourists or short-term visitors, securing bail might be more complicated, especially if the authorities consider the risk of fleeing the jurisdiction.

In practice, the UAE's bail system aims to balance the rights of the accused with public safety and the efficient administration of justice. Because legal procedures can vary by emirate and case specifics, those facing charges should seek legal advice immediately to understand their options regarding bail. Visitors arrested in the UAE are advised to contact their embassy or consulate promptly, as these offices can sometimes help facilitate communication with lawyers and clarify bail procedures.

Complaints Against Police

The police force in the UAE is generally seen as **efficient, professional, and focused on maintaining safety and public order.** The government invests heavily in training and modern technology, which helps uphold this reputation. However, despite this positive view, some complaints do arise, particularly from residents and foreign nationals.

Common complaints against the police often involve allegations of **excessive force during arrests, mistreatment or delays in communication,** and occasional **concerns about fairness in procedures.** Foreigners sometimes report difficulties understanding their rights or navigating the legal process, especially due to language barriers. There are also complaints related to strict enforcement of public morality laws.

If you want to file a complaint against the police in the UAE, you can do so through official channels. Each emirate has dedicated police complaint departments. Complaints can be submitted in person at police stations, online through official police websites, or via the Ministry of Interior's hotline.

The UAE has limited independent bodies handling police complaints. International groups like **Amnesty International** (https://www.amnesty.org) and **Human Rights Watch** (https://www.hrw.org) monitor the country but do not intervene in individual cases. For personal assistance, embassies or consulates can offer some guidance or support.

In summary, while the UAE police are mostly respected for their professionalism, complaints do occur, and there are official ways to report concerns, though options for independent external review remain limited.

General Questions

1. ***If I am convicted in the UAE, am I likely to be released on bail pending the outcome of my appeal?*** If you are convicted in the UAE, being released on bail pending the outcome of your appeal is generally possible but not guaranteed. The decision to grant bail during the appeals process is at the discretion of the court and depends on factors such as the nature and seriousness of the offense, the risk of flight, and whether public safety might be compromised. For serious crimes, especially those involving violence, drugs, or security concerns, courts are less likely to

grant bail. Foreign nationals may face additional scrutiny due to concerns about them leaving the country before the appeal concludes. It's important to consult a local lawyer who can advise based on the specifics of your case and help petition the court for bail if appropriate.

2. ***Who is entitled to bail?*** In the UAE, anyone accused or convicted of a crime may be entitled to bail, but it is not an automatic right. Bail eligibility depends on several factors, including the seriousness of the offense, the likelihood that the accused will flee, and whether their release could threaten public safety or interfere with the investigation. Generally, bail is more likely to be granted for less serious crimes and to individuals who have strong ties to the country, such as residents or citizens. For serious offenses like terrorism, drug trafficking, or violent crimes, bail is often denied. Ultimately, the decision rests with the judge, who evaluates each case individually before granting or denying bail.

3. ***If I am arrested, how soon will I see a judge or magistrate?*** If you are arrested in the UAE, you will typically be brought before a judge or magistrate **within 48 hours** of your detention. This is the maximum legal period authorities are allowed to hold someone without judicial review. During this initial hearing, the judge will review the arrest, decide whether to extend your detention, grant bail, or order your release. It's important to request legal counsel as early as possible to ensure your rights are protected during this process.

4. ***Will I be able to contact my country's embassy in the UAE?*** **Yes.** If you are arrested in the UAE, you have the right to contact your country's embassy or consulate. Authorities are generally required to inform your embassy of your detention if you request it. The embassy can provide consular assistance, such as visiting you in detention, helping you understand the local legal process, offering a list of local lawyers, and ensuring your welfare is protected. While embassies cannot interfere in legal proceedings or secure your release, they play an important role in supporting their nationals abroad. It's advisable to ask to contact your embassy as soon as possible after your arrest.

CHAPTER 11

JAILS VS. PRISONS: CONDITIONS & CULTURE

IN THIS CHAPTER

- Overview
- Prison Conditions and Living Environment
- Inmate Rights and Legal Protections
- General Questions

CHAPTER 11

JAILS VS. PRISONS: CONDITIONS & CULTURE

Overview

In the UAE, the prison system is structured to distinguish between jails and prisons based largely on the length and nature of sentences, similar to many other countries. **Jails**, often **referred to as detention centers or police lockups**, are primarily used for short-term detention, such as holding suspects during investigation or for sentences typically less than one year. **Prisons**, on the other hand, house inmates serving longer sentences after conviction.

Jails and prisons in the UAE are operated **under the supervision of the Ministry of Interior and the Federal Authority for Identity and Citizenship**, with each emirate managing its own facilities under federal guidelines. The system emphasizes security, order, and discipline, with modern facilities in larger emirates like Dubai and Abu Dhabi that incorporate advanced technology and infrastructure. Smaller or more remote facilities may have more basic conditions. The UAE also segregates inmates **by gender, nationality**, and **the type of offense to maintain order and safety**.

One of the biggest challenges in the UAE prison system is balancing security and humane treatment while managing a **highly diverse inmate population**, which includes many foreign nationals from various cultural backgrounds. Language barriers and differing legal expectations can complicate communication and access to services. Another challenge is addressing the **mental health and rehabilitation** needs of inmates within a system traditionally focused on punishment and deterrence.

Rehabilitation programs in the UAE are increasingly becoming part of the correctional approach. These programs include vocational training, religious and educational courses, and counseling aimed at reintegration into society. Some facilities offer skills development in trades such as carpentry, sewing, and computer literacy. Psychological support and addiction treatment programs are also available in some prisons, reflecting a growing recognition of the importance of rehabilitation over purely punitive measures. However, the extent and availability of these programs can vary by emirate and facility.

Prison Conditions and Living Environment

In the UAE, prison conditions vary somewhat between emirates and facilities, but overall, the prison system is **highly structured** and **security-focused**. Inmates are housed in units based on classification, which takes into account the nature of the crime, sentence length, behavior, and nationality. Facilities typically separate prisoners by gender, and in many cases, by religion or nationality, especially in larger cities like Dubai and Abu Dhabi. Security levels range from minimum to maximum, and classification determines not only housing but also access to programs and privileges.

Access to health care in UAE prisons is guaranteed by law, and most facilities provide **basic medical services** through in-house clinics. These clinics typically handle routine care, emergency treatment, and chronic conditions. However, challenges remain, especially when it comes to specialist care, mental health services, and timely treatment. Language barriers and the high percentage of foreign inmates—many of whom are labor migrants—can complicate communication and limit patients' understanding of their treatment options. Inmates sometimes report delays in receiving adequate care or medication, especially in less-developed facilities.

Food, sanitation, and basic needs in UAE prisons are **generally adequate by regional standards**, but conditions can feel strict and institutional. Meals are provided at set times and follow basic nutritional guidelines. That said, the food may not always meet the dietary or cultural preferences of a diverse inmate population. Sanitation varies by facility: newer prisons tend to offer better hygiene and more modern infrastructure, while older or more crowded facilities may face issues such as limited access to hot water or clean toilets. Prisoners are typically given basic hygiene items like soap and toothpaste, but they may need to purchase other personal goods through commissaries or rely on family support.

While conditions are orderly and controlled, the environment is often described as highly regimented, with an emphasis on discipline and obedience. Nonetheless, the government has made ongoing efforts to improve prison conditions, especially in larger emirates, and continues to promote rehabilitation alongside security.

Inmate Rights and Legal Protections

In the United Arab Emirates, inmates do have certain legal rights and protections, although the **system tends to prioritize state security, discipline, and public order over individual liberties.** The UAE Constitution and various federal laws provide a legal framework intended to protect the rights of prisoners, but enforcement and access to these rights can vary significantly depending on the nature of the crime, the inmate's nationality, and the facility.

Constitutionally, prisoners in the UAE are **guaranteed dignity and humane treatment.** Article 26 of the UAE Constitution explicitly states that no person shall be subjected to torture or degrading treatment. In practice, this means inmates have the right to safe and sanitary conditions, access to food and medical care, and the ability to practice their religion. However, because the legal system incorporates elements of Sharia law and emphasizes public morality, the scope of prisoner rights is more limited than in many Western countries.

Access to **legal resources and court appeals** is provided under UAE law. Prisoners have the right to appeal their convictions and request legal counsel. Defense lawyers may visit clients in prison, and translation services are often available for non-Arabic speakers, though their quality can vary. However, access to legal materials is limited. Unlike in some countries, prisons in the UAE do not typically offer legal libraries or widespread self-help legal resources. Most inmates rely on outside legal counsel or embassy assistance to navigate the appeals process.

Issues of abuse—whether physical, psychological, or procedural—have been reported, especially in cases involving foreign nationals, political detainees, or individuals accused of serious crimes. International human rights organizations such as Amnesty International and Human Rights Watch have raised concerns about detainees being held incommunicado, denied access to legal counsel during interrogation, or subjected to harsh conditions. While such reports do not represent the experience of all inmates, they highlight systemic challenges within the prison and justice system.

Legal recourse for inmates who experience abuse exists in theory, but pursuing justice from inside prison can be difficult. Complaints can be submitted to prison authorities, the public prosecution office, or the courts, but success often depends on the availability of evidence, the willingness of officials to investigate, and the inmate's access to legal support. Foreign inmates are encouraged to contact their embassy or consulate if they believe their rights are being violated, as diplomatic channels may offer additional pressure or advocacy.

General Questions

1. ***What is the difference between a jail and prison in the UAE?***
   In the UAE, jails are short-term detention centers typically used for holding individuals under investigation, awaiting trial, or serving sentences under one year. They are often located near

police stations and are more temporary in nature. Prisons, by contrast, are long-term facilities for those convicted and sentenced to extended terms. Managed by the Ministry of Interior, prisons are more structured, separating inmates by gender, offense, and sometimes nationality, and may offer limited rehabilitation programs. **The key difference lies in the duration and purpose of confinement.**

2. ***Do jails and prisons offer religious services to inmates?*** **Yes.** Jails and prisons in the UAE generally offer religious services to inmates, particularly for the Muslim population. Islamic practices are respected and supported, with access to prayer areas, Qur'ans, and religious guidance. During Ramadan, inmates are typically allowed to fast and attend special prayers. For non-Muslim inmates, the extent of religious accommodation can vary by facility. While some prisons may allow private worship or visits from clergy of other faiths, these services are more limited and depend on the prison's policies and resources.

3. ***How do prisoners spend their time?*** In UAE prisons, inmates spend their time under a structured daily routine focused on discipline, order, and limited rehabilitation. Most of the day is spent in their cells, with scheduled times for meals, prayer, and outdoor recreation. Some prisons offer vocational training, religious classes, and basic education programs aimed at rehabilitation. Inmates may also have access to television, reading materials, or light work duties, depending on their classification and behavior. However, activities are generally restricted, and access to programs can vary widely between facilities.

4. ***How does the prison commissary system work in the UAE?*** In the UAE, the prison commissary system allows inmates to purchase basic personal items such as toiletries, snacks, phone cards, and sometimes limited clothing or stationery. Each inmate is usually given an account that can be funded by family members or, in some cases, by the inmate's own earnings from prison work. Purchases are made from a designated shop inside the facility on specific days. Prices and available items can vary depending on the prison, and inmates are often limited in what

and how much they can buy. Access to the commissary is considered a privilege and may depend on an inmate's behavior or classification.

5. ***What type of medical care do prisoners receive?*** In the UAE, prisoners are legally entitled to medical care, with each prison typically having a clinic for routine treatment and basic health needs. For serious conditions, inmates may be taken to government hospitals. While care includes physical and mental health services, access can be inconsistent, with some reports of delays, limited mental health support, and poor hygiene. Non-citizen inmates may face added challenges like language barriers, but denying essential medical care can lead to legal consequences.

6. ***What is prison culture like in the UAE?*** Prison culture in the UAE is generally **strict and disciplined**, reflecting the country's conservative social norms and legal system. Inmates are expected to follow rigid rules, with limited personal freedoms and close supervision. Respect for authority is strongly enforced, and there is little tolerance for dissent or disorder. Social interactions among prisoners tend to be cautious and reserved, often shaped by cultural, tribal, or nationality lines. Religious practices, especially Islam, play a significant role in daily life and help shape routines and behavior. While some facilities strive to maintain order and rehabilitation programs, overall, the environment can be tense, with a focus on security and control.

CHAPTER 12

HELPING A FRIEND OR RELATIVE IMPRISONED IN THE UAE

IN THIS CHAPTER

- Overview
- Sending Food, Supplies, and Money to an Inmate
- Mail, Phone Calls, and Visitation
- Prison Scams
- Upon Release

CHAPTER 12

HELPING A FRIEND OR RELATIVE IMPRISONED IN THE UAE

Overview

If a family member or loved one is imprisoned in the UAE, the first step is to stay calm and gather as much information as possible about their situation, including charges, location, and legal status. Contact the local police or prison authorities to confirm details, and **immediately reach out to your country's embassy or consulate in the UAE** for assistance. Embassies can provide guidance, monitor the case, and help ensure the prisoner's rights are respected, though they cannot intervene in legal proceedings directly. Hiring a local lawyer experienced in UAE law is crucial to navigate the legal system effectively.

It's important to respect local customs and laws, avoid public criticism of authorities, and communicate carefully to prevent jeopardizing the case. Sending money or parcels usually requires approval from prison authorities, so check regulations beforehand. Staying patient and persistent while maintaining regular contact with legal counsel and the embassy can make a significant difference in supporting your imprisoned relative or friend.

Sending Food, Supplies, and Money to an Inmate

In the UAE, family and friends **generally cannot bring outside food directly to inmates** in prisons or jails because food is provided by the facility under strict hygiene and security controls. This helps prevent smuggling and contamination. While some prisons might allow small snacks or gifts during official visits, this depends on the specific facility and requires prior approval from prison authorities.

Sending packages to inmates is **allowed but heavily regulated.** Typically, only essential items like personal hygiene products, approved clothing, and letters are permitted. Prohibited items include electronics, sharp objects, drugs, or anything that could threaten security. All packages undergo thorough inspection and must be approved by prison officials before delivery to the prisoner.

To send money, family and friends usually **use official channels through the prison administration or designated bank accounts**. Direct cash transfers to inmates are generally not accepted. Instead, funds are deposited into the inmate's account, which they can use to buy items from the prison commissary or cover other approved expenses. You can use international bank transfers or services like Western Union, including the inmate's full name and ID. Some paperwork may be required, so check in advance. After sending, confirm with the prison or embassy that the funds were received to ensure your loved one can access the money. **It's important to contact the specific prison to understand their exact procedures, limits, and required documentation to ensure the money or packages reach the inmate smoothly.**

Mail, Phone Calls, and Visitation

Inmates in UAE prisons are generally allowed to receive and send mail, but **all correspondence is carefully monitored and screened** by prison authorities to prevent the exchange of prohibited content, such as plans for escape, threats, or contraband instructions. Mail can be delayed or censored, and some sensitive topics may be restricted. Sending letters is an important way for prisoners to maintain contact with family and legal representatives, but security concerns mean privacy is limited.

Possession of **personal cell phones** is **strictly forbidden** in UAE prisons. Inmates do not have access to mobile phones and cannot receive calls on them. However, prisoners may be allowed to make phone calls using prison landlines or monitored phones under supervision, often limited to calls to immediate family or legal counsel. These calls are typically restricted in frequency and duration, and the exact rules vary by facility. Receiving incoming calls is generally not allowed to maintain security and prevent unauthorized communication.

Visiting rights in UAE prisons are generally **reserved for close family members**, such as spouses, parents, children, and sometimes legal representatives. Visits are **scheduled in advance** and are subject to approval by prison authorities. The number of visits and their length are limited, often to once or twice a month, with strict time limits. Visitors must comply with security procedures, including presenting valid identification, passing security checks, and adhering to dress codes that respect local cultural norms. Physical contact may be limited or prohibited during visits, and all interactions are closely monitored.

Prison Scams

Unfortunately, scams involving prisoners do occur in the UAE. These often involve **fraudsters posing as inmates** or their relatives, claiming urgent needs for money due to medical emergencies, legal fees, or threats of extended sentences unless bribes are paid. They may use emotional stories or pressure tactics to convince you to send money quickly. Some scammers offer **fake legal help or bail services**, promising early release or reduced sentences if you pay upfront, but they never deliver any assistance. Others might **impersonate prison officials or lawyers** to trick families into sharing personal information or documents, which can then be used for identity theft or fraud. There are also scams where people pretend to be prison staff demanding payment to arrange visits, phone calls, or send parcels, even though these services are usually free or managed through official channels.

Red flags to watch for include unexpected requests for money, insistence on secrecy, refusal to provide verifiable details, inconsistent stories, and pressure to act immediately. Scammers may also ask you to use unofficial money transfer methods or gift cards.

To avoid falling victim, it's important to **verify any offers or requests** through trusted sources like embassies or licensed attorneys, and never share sensitive information or send money without confirming the legitimacy of the request. If you suspect you're being scammed, do not send any money or personal information. Verify the situation through official channels such as your embassy, the prison administration, or local law enforcement. Report any suspicious contacts to authorities promptly to help prevent others from falling victim. Staying cautious and confirming all information can protect you from these common scams.

Upon Release

When a foreigner is released from prison in the UAE, there are often strict rules and legal obligations that come into play. In many cases, the authorities impose **deportation** or **immediate exit orders**, especially if the offense is considered serious or related to criminal activity. This means the person must leave the country soon after release and may be banned from returning for several years. Even if deportation is not automatic, many former inmates face travel bans that restrict their ability to leave or re-enter the UAE for a specified period.

Beyond travel restrictions, released foreigners may be **required to report regularly to immigration or police authorities** for monitoring or follow-up. There might also be probation-like conditions that they need to fulfill, such as refraining from certain activities, maintaining good behavior, or staying in a specific area. Additionally, there could be **financial obligations**, including payment of fines, restitution to victims, or court-ordered compensations. Sometimes, released individuals face limitations on employment, especially if their conviction relates to fraud, drugs, or other sensitive sectors.

Navigating these post-release conditions can be complex, particularly for foreigners unfamiliar with the legal system and local customs. It is highly recommended that released inmates consult with a local lawyer or their country's embassy to fully understand their rights and responsibilities. This legal guidance can help avoid further violations that could lead to re-arrest, fines, or extended bans.

CHAPTER 13

THE ADMINISTRATION OF JUSTICE

IN THIS CHAPTER

- UAE's Legal System
- General Questions
- Law of the Land True Story
- Takeaways

CHAPTER 13

THE ADMINISTRATION OF JUSTICE

UAE's Legal System

The legal system of the United Arab Emirates is deeply rooted in the country's history, which before 1971 was governed mainly by tribal customs and Islamic law. When the UAE was formed as a federation of seven emirates, it established a **federal constitution** that made Islam and Sharia law the primary foundations of its legal framework. This system uniquely blends **traditional Islamic principles with civil law influences** borrowed from countries like Egypt and France. **Sharia law** primarily governs **personal status matters for Muslims**, such as marriage, divorce, inheritance, and family law, while **civil codes** regulate **commercial transactions, contracts, property, and criminal offenses.** Federal laws apply broadly across most emirates; however, emirates such as Abu Dhabi, Dubai, and Ras al-Khaimah have their own local court systems and legislative authority, which adds complexity to the legal landscape.

The judiciary is structured into different levels, with **federal courts** handling most cases and **local courts** operating independently in some emirates. There are also special courts within free zones like **the Dubai International Financial Centre** (**DIFC**) and **Abu Dhabi Global Market** (**ADGM**), which operate under common law principles and use English as the official language, catering mainly to international business disputes.

Judges in the UAE are **appointed by rulers or executive authorities**, and unlike many Western systems, **there is no jury trial**. The legal process involves **trial courts, appeals courts**, and ultimately the highest courts such as the **Federal Supreme Court** or **local courts of cassation**, depending on the emirate. Arbitration and mediation are encouraged, especially in commercial matters, to provide more flexible and efficient dispute resolution.

Despite these features, the UAE's legal system faces **some challenges**. Judicial independence can sometimes be limited because judges are appointed by the ruling authorities, raising concerns about impartiality in politically sensitive cases. The system's complexity, with overlapping federal and local laws, can cause confusion and inconsistency, especially for expatriates and foreign businesses. Transparency and access to evidence in criminal and civil proceedings may also be restricted. Personal status laws based on Sharia sometimes result in gender inequalities, particularly regarding inheritance rights and child custody, which reflect traditional interpretations of Islamic law. Additionally, delays in the court process and language barriers, since proceedings may be in Arabic, can affect timely and fair access to justice.

In recent years, the UAE has introduced a **series of legal reforms aimed at modernizing the system** and aligning it more closely with international standards. Harsh corporal punishments such as flogging and stoning have been abolished. Civil marriage options have been introduced for non-Muslims, allowing greater personal freedom. While the UAE traditionally prohibits consensual cohabitation (unmarried couples living together), in recent years, laws have been relaxed to decriminalize cohabitation and extramarital relationships, provided no complaint is filed by either party. Although technically still illegal, enforcement has become more lenient, especially for foreigners and expatriates, and authorities generally do not intervene unless there is a public disturbance or formal complaint.

Additionally, the government has also strengthened legal protections for children and families, signaling a shift toward more progressive policies. These changes reflect the UAE's efforts to balance its Islamic legal heritage with the needs of a rapidly developing, multicultural society and a dynamic global economy.

Overall, **the UAE legal system is a unique blend of tradition and modernity,** aiming to preserve cultural and religious values while supporting a business-friendly and diverse environment. Understanding its structure and nuances is essential for anyone living in or engaging with the country legally, socially, or commercially.

General Questions

1. ***Will the court treat first-time offenders and tourists with more leniency?*** **Depends.** The treatment of first-time offenders and tourists is discretionary, meaning judges consider factors like the nature of the offense, the individual's background, and any mitigating circumstances before deciding whether to show leniency. This allows the court to tailor its response rather than applying a fixed rule, so outcomes can vary. The UAE legal system does tend to show more leniency toward first-time offenders and tourists, especially for minor offenses. Recent reforms offer alternatives to imprisonment like fines and rehabilitation programs, particularly for non-violent crimes such as drug use. Courts now have discretion to avoid mandatory deportation for first-time offenders. Dubai even has specialized courts to quickly handle minor tourist offenses, allowing faster resolution. However, the system remains strict on serious offenses, and leniency depends on the case and judicial discretion, so it's not guaranteed.

2. ***If I am charged with a crime, which court is likely to hear my case?*** In the UAE, the court that hears your case depends on several factors, including the type of crime, where it happened, and whether the case is criminal or civil. Generally, minor criminal offenses and first-time cases start in the **Court of First Instance**, which handles trials at the initial level. More serious crimes may be tried in **criminal courts** at this level. If your case is in Dubai, Abu Dhabi, or Ras al-Khaimah, local courts there may handle it instead of federal courts. For commercial disputes, especially in free zones like the Dubai International Financial Centre (DIFC),

specialized courts using common law principles may hear the case. If you are unsure, it's important to consult a local lawyer who can clarify which court has jurisdiction over your specific situation.

3. ***What is the standard of proof in a criminal case in the UAE?*** In the UAE, the standard of proof in a criminal case is generally **"beyond a reasonable doubt."** This means the prosecution must provide enough clear and convincing evidence to convince the court that the accused is guilty to a high degree of certainty. The court carefully examines witness testimony, documents, and other evidence before reaching a verdict. If there is any reasonable doubt about the accused's guilt, the court is expected to acquit. This standard aligns with many international legal systems to ensure fairness in criminal trials.

Law of the Land True Story[21]

The execution of Shahzadi Khan, a 33-year-old Indian woman in Abu Dhabi, sheds light on the challenges foreigners may face in the UAE's legal system. Accused of murdering her employer's four-month-old child in 2022, Shahzadi was sentenced to death after what her family claims was an unfair trial. Despite recommendations for a post-mortem, the child's parents waived further investigation. A year later, a video surfaced allegedly showing Shahzadi confessing—though her family says it was made under pressure and abuse.

Her father, who fought for two years to save her, argued that she was inadequately represented and denied a fair defense. The case was upheld by the UAE's highest court, the Court of Cassation, and the execution was carried out on February 15, 2025. The Indian government had filed mercy petitions, but they were ultimately unsuccessful. News

21 https://www.thehindu.com/news/national/indian-woman-on-death-row-in-abu-dhabi-executed-delhi-high-court-told/article69285768.ece

of her death only reached the family after the fact, devastating her father and raising questions about transparency and due process.

This case illustrates key features of the UAE's legal system: strict penalties for serious crimes, limited judicial discretion for lower-income defendants, and swift legal proceedings. While the UAE has made reforms in areas like personal status and drug law, capital punishment and forced confessions remain critical concerns—especially for migrant workers unfamiliar with the legal process. Shahzadi's case underscores the importance of legal awareness and support for those working abroad in high-stakes environments.

Takeaways

The UAE's legal system is a hybrid of Islamic Sharia law (governing personal status matters for Muslims) and civil law influences (covering commercial, criminal, and property laws). Federal laws apply across the country, but some emirates have independent local courts, adding legal complexity.

The court system includes federal courts, local emirate-level courts, and specialized common-law courts in free zones. There is no jury system, and judges are appointed by rulers. The system includes trial courts, appeals courts, and courts of cassation for final review.

The UAE has recently reformed laws around civil rights, cohabitation, and alternatives to prison for first-time offenders. Judges have wide discretion, and leniency may be granted to tourists or minor offenders, though serious crimes like murder still result in severe penalties, including the death sentence.

Critics point to limited judicial independence, language barriers, and lack of transparency in criminal cases. Foreigners may face unfair trials if they lack strong legal representation. Confessions allegedly extracted under duress and delays in communication with families, as seen in the Shahzadi Khan case, reveal systemic weaknesses.

CHAPTER 14

CRIME VICTIM ASSISTANCE

IN THIS CHAPTER

- Overview
- What to Do If You Are the Victim of a Crime
- Common Tourist Scams in the UAE
- Consular Assistance
- General Questions

CHAPTER 14

CRIME VICTIM ASSISTANCE

Overview

Crime victim assistance in the UAE has grown in recent years, with both government and non-government resources now available to support those affected. Each emirate has specific departments within the police and judicial systems dedicated to helping victims navigate legal, emotional, and logistical challenges following a crime. For example, Dubai Police offer a **Victim Support Program** that provides information, updates on case status, and emotional support. **Abu Dhabi Judicial Department** operates a similar victim and witness assistance service. These programs often include translators, legal guidance, and social workers to help non-Arabic speakers or vulnerable individuals. **Ajman**, **Umm Al Quwain**, and **Fujairah** offer victim support primarily through their local police departments. While these programs may be smaller in scale, they still provide basic services such as case updates, medical referrals, translation help, and support during legal proceedings. Victims are encouraged to report crimes at the nearest police station, where officers trained in victim-sensitive procedures are generally available.

In Sharjah, the **Sharjah Social Services Department** (**SSSD**) plays a major role in providing care and protection to vulnerable individuals, including crime victims. They operate shelters for women and children, offer psychological counseling, and help with legal referrals. Victims of domestic abuse or trafficking can also access emergency housing and crisis intervention through the department. **Ras Al Khaimah** has a growing legal and social support network. The RAK Police and RAK Courts provide dedicated services for victims of violence and family disputes, and there are partnerships with local social welfare agencies for psychological support. Additionally, across all emirates, **public prosecutors' offices** play an important role in informing victims of their rights and helping them file official complaints. Many emirates also have **family guidance sections** within their court systems, especially in cases involving domestic violence or family conflict.

In addition to official services, some **non-governmental organizations (NGOs)** and **embassies** also assist crime victims, particularly expats. Shelters and advocacy groups, like the **Dubai Foundation for Women and Children**, offer support for victims of domestic abuse and trafficking.[22] Embassies can help with legal referrals, emergency travel documents, or contact with local authorities. For financial crimes, **UAE Central Bank** may provide guidance on reporting fraud and pursuing restitution.

For emergencies, residents and visitors can contact **999** for **police assistance** or **998** for **ambulance services**. Victims are encouraged to report crimes promptly at local police stations or through online reporting systems in some emirates. The UAE takes crimes—especially those involving violence, exploitation, or abuse—seriously and offers confidential reporting options to ensure the safety and dignity of the victim.

What to Do If You Are the Victim of a Crime

If you are the victim of a crime in the United Arab Emirates (UAE), your first priority should be ensuring your immediate safety. If you are in danger, call the police by dialing 999, which is the general emergency number across the country. You should also try to get to a safe location, such as a nearby hotel, police station, embassy, or a public area with people around.

22 https://www.dfwac.ae

Once you are safe, you should **report the crime to the police** as soon as possible. You can do this by visiting the nearest police station, many of which have English-speaking officers, especially in larger emirates like Dubai and Abu Dhabi. You can also report certain crimes online using the Dubai Police app or website[23], or through the Abu Dhabi Police portal[24]. Dubai also has **Smart Police Stations (SPS)** that are open 24/7 and allow you to report incidents without needing to speak directly to an officer.

If you were physically harmed or sexually assaulted, you should **seek medical attention immediately**. Hospitals can provide treatment and collect forensic evidence, which may be critical to your case. Be aware that some hospitals might ask for a police report before offering treatment for certain types of injuries. Public hospitals provide emergency services regardless of your nationality, although follow-up care may depend on your insurance or ability to pay.

As mentioned above, victim support services in the UAE vary by emirate. In Dubai, for example, the **Dubai Foundation for Women and Children** offers shelter, legal aid, and psychological counseling for victims of abuse, domestic violence, and human trafficking. You can contact them via their website at https://www.dfwac.ae or call their hotline at 800-111. Dubai Police also runs a **Victim Support Program** that can assist with counseling and legal referrals. In Abu Dhabi, the **Social Support Centers** under the Ministry of Interior help victims of family violence and other crimes. They can be reached at 800-5354 or through https://www.moi.gov.ae.

If you are a foreign national, you should also **contact your embassy or consulate** for help. They can assist you in contacting local authorities, provide information about legal rights, help you find a lawyer or translator, and offer emergency aid such as shelter or repatriation if needed. You can find a list of embassies in the UAE at **https://www.mofa.gov.ae/en/missions/foreign-missions-in-uae.**

23 https://www.dubaipolice.gov.ae

24 https://www.adpolice.gov.ae

Legal representation is strongly advised, especially in more serious cases. UAE law allows you to hire a licensed attorney, and having one can help you navigate the country's legal system, which can be complex and has very different norms compared to many Western countries. This is especially important in sensitive cases involving sexual assault or moral conduct, where certain behaviors (such as drinking or being alone with someone of the opposite sex) may unintentionally complicate your legal position.

It's also important to know your rights and limitations under UAE law. Authorities generally protect the identity of victims, particularly in court proceedings. However, filing a false report is a criminal offense, so it's critical to be truthful and clear when giving your account. Due to cultural and religious laws, public discussion of certain crimes—especially those involving sex, alcohol, or personal conduct—should be handled carefully and always with legal guidance.

You can also seek **private counseling services,** which are widely available in major cities. These services are offered by licensed psychologists, psychiatrists, and clinical social workers who often speak English and other widely spoken languages. To find private counseling, you can start by searching online for licensed clinics and mental health centers. Websites like https://www.doh.gov.ae (Abu Dhabi Department of Health) and https://www.dha.gov.ae (Dubai Health Authority) list accredited healthcare providers, including mental health professionals. You can also use platforms like https://hoopfull.com to search for therapists by specialty, language, and location.

Many hospitals in the UAE also have outpatient psychiatry and psychology departments. Reputable facilities like **Cleveland Clinic Abu Dhabi**, **American Hospital Dubai**, and **Mediclinic** offer therapy sessions for trauma, anxiety, and post-crime stress. International medical centers often provide services tailored for expats and offer confidential consultations.

If you are employed, check if your company offers an **Employee Assistance Program** (**EAP**). These programs often include free or subsidized access to mental health services, either on-site or through referral to a local clinic. In some cases, embassies may also maintain a list of recommended counselors or psychologists who speak your language and are familiar with helping foreign nationals in distress. When choosing a provider, make sure they are **licensed by the UAE health authorities** and ask about their experience working with trauma or crime victims. You can also request a female or male therapist depending on your comfort level. Most sessions are paid out-of-pocket unless covered by private insurance, so be sure to inquire about fees in advance.

Being the victim of a crime in the UAE can be a frightening and overwhelming experience, particularly for foreigners unfamiliar with the local system. However, by taking prompt action, reporting the incident through the proper channels, and seeking legal and emotional support, you can protect yourself and take steps toward justice and recovery.

Common Tourist Scams in the UAE

Although the United Arab Emirates (UAE) is generally considered safe and well-policed, tourists—especially in popular destinations like Dubai and Abu Dhabi—may still encounter scams. These are typically non-violent and rely more on deception or manipulation than outright theft. Below is a guide to common scams targeting tourists, red flags to look out for, and how to protect yourself.

One of the most common scams is the **"overpriced taxi" scam**, where unlicensed drivers approach tourists at airports, malls, or popular attractions and offer a ride—often claiming it will be cheaper or faster. These taxis don't use meters, and once you reach your destination, you're quoted a high fare. To avoid this, always use official taxis. Look for the tan-colored cars with roof signs, or book through government-approved apps like **Careem** or **Uber**, which are regulated and offer fare estimates upfront.

Another popular trick is the **"tour package scam."** This typically happens online or near tourist hotspots, where individuals offer deals on desert safaris, yacht rentals, or city tours at too-good-to-be-true prices. Victims either never get the tour or find the service to be fake or substandard. To protect yourself, only book through established operators with verified websites and reviews. Avoid giving deposits in cash or to individuals who can't provide a business license or receipt.

"Friendly stranger" or distraction scams can also occur, especially in crowded areas like souks (markets), beaches, or metro stations. Someone might bump into you or try to engage you in conversation, giving an accomplice the chance to snatch your wallet or phone. Another version involves someone offering unsolicited help with directions, tickets, or ATMs while watching for your PIN or stealing your card. The red flag here is overly friendly or persistent strangers offering unsolicited help. Be polite but cautious, and keep valuables close—preferably in a front-facing bag or a money belt.

Tourists may also encounter the **"luxury goods scam"** at fake or gray-market shops selling counterfeit perfumes, watches, electronics, or designer clothing. These stores often look legitimate and may even be located in malls, but the products are of poor quality or entirely fake. If someone is pushing you to buy quickly or offering an unbelievable deal, it's a warning sign. To avoid this, shop only at official retail stores or major mall outlets and always ask for a receipt with return details.

A more recent scam involves **fraudulent rental listings**, particularly if you're booking a vacation apartment in advance through lesser-known platforms or private Facebook groups. Scammers may post beautiful photos of a non-existent or unavailable property, take your payment, and then disappear. Always use reputable sites like **Airbnb**, **Booking.com**, or **official hotel websites**, and never wire money or pay through untraceable services.

In rare cases, some scammers use **romance or companionship ploys** to target solo travelers. This could involve someone approaching you in a club, hotel lobby, or online dating app, leading to a situation where you're pressured to buy expensive drinks, gifts, or even give up personal details. These situations can quickly turn into blackmail or theft. Be wary of fast-moving relationships and never hand over your passport, phone, or wallet.

To stay safe, **trust your instincts.** If something feels rushed, shady, or too convenient, step away. Use official apps, government-regulated transport, and well-reviewed businesses. Be discreet with valuables and avoid flashing large amounts of cash or expensive items in public. Most importantly, know that you can always contact the police by dialing **999** or, in Dubai, reach out through their **non-emergency services** on **901** for tourist-specific inquiries.

Consular Assistance

If you become the victim of a crime while in the United Arab Emirates (UAE), your country's embassy or consulate can be a **critical source of support.** While they cannot replace local police or override the UAE legal system, consular officials are there to assist you through the process, help you understand your rights, and ensure you're treated fairly under local law.

One of the first things an embassy can do is help you **contact the local police and file a report.** If there are language barriers or confusion about procedures, consular staff can guide you or arrange translation assistance. While they won't physically intervene in the investigation, they can accompany you to police stations or hospitals in certain cases or help ensure that due process is followed.

Embassies can also provide you with a **list of local lawyers** who are licensed to practice in the UAE. This is especially important if the crime is serious, such as assault, sexual violence, or fraud, or if you're unsure how to respond to questioning. They can't give you legal advice themselves, but they can point you toward someone who can.

If you are injured or in shock, consular officials can help arrange **medical treatment** by referring you to hospitals or clinics. They may also assist with notifying your family or friends back home if you give permission to do so. In extreme situations—such as if your passport is stolen or you are without money or shelter due to the crime—they may offer emergency travel documents, coordinate temporary lodging through charities, or provide contact with your home country's support agencies.

Embassies often maintain lists of counseling services, translators, or victim support organizations in the region. While the UAE itself does not have a widespread public system for victim assistance, consulates sometimes work with local NGOs or religious institutions to offer support to nationals in distress.

General Questions

1. ***If I am a victim of a crime, can I legally be compensated?*** **Yes.** However, the process depends on the nature of the crime and the outcome of any criminal proceedings. Compensation is not automatic, and you must take specific legal steps to pursue it. Under UAE law, crime victims can file a **civil claim** for financial compensation as part of the **criminal trial** or through a **separate civil lawsuit**. This is most common in cases involving physical injury, emotional distress, property damage, or financial loss. If the accused is convicted, the court may award **"diya"** (**blood money**) or **financial damages**, especially in cases of personal injury or death. In other cases, the judge may award compensation based on documented losses or medical costs. For example, in an assault case, if the offender is convicted, the court may sentence the person and also order them to pay you damages. In a fraud or theft case, you may be able to recover stolen funds or property if it's traceable and recoverable. However, there is **no government victim compensation fund** in the UAE similar to those in some Western countries. Compensation is typically the responsibility of the convicted offender, and if they are unable or unwilling to pay, collecting damages can be difficult.

2. ***If a family member falls victim to homicide, can I bring the body back to my home country?*** **Yes.** If a family member is a homicide victim in the UAE, you can usually repatriate the body to your home country. This can only happen after the police complete their investigation and the authorities issue the

required documents like the death certificate and a no objection certificate. Your embassy can assist you with the paperwork and coordinate with local officials, while a licensed funeral home will handle the body's preparation and transport.

3. ***What protections are in place to ensure the safety and confidentiality of crime victims during legal proceedings?*** In the UAE, crime victims are protected by laws that aim to ensure their safety and maintain confidentiality during legal proceedings. The authorities generally keep the identity of victims confidential, especially in sensitive cases like sexual assault or family violence, to protect their privacy and dignity. Courts may hold closed sessions to prevent public disclosure of personal details. Victims are also protected from retaliation or intimidation by the accused, with police and prosecutors able to impose restraining orders or other measures as needed. Additionally, victims have the right to legal representation and support throughout the process. While victim protection is recognized, the level of support and confidentiality can vary depending on the case and emirate, so victims often benefit from legal counsel to help safeguard their rights during the proceedings.

CHAPTER 15

POLICE

IN THIS CHAPTER

- Overview
- Police Response
- Police and Community Relations
- Police Use of Force
- Law of the Land True Story

CHAPTER 15

POLICE

Overview

The structure of the police force in the UAE is distinctive in that it merges centralized federal oversight with localized emirate-level authority. At the top of the hierarchy is the **Ministry of Interior**, which plays a unifying role in coordinating law enforcement activities across all seven emirates. It oversees **national security, criminal justice standards, immigration control, and corrections.** However, actual policing within each emirate is carried out by individual police departments that operate semi-autonomously. Each emirate has **its own police force** responsible for handling **local law enforcement, public safety, traffic management, cybercrime, and internal security.** These forces ultimately report to both their respective rulers and the federal Ministry of Interior, creating a dual accountability structure that reflects the UAE's federal system. Within each emirate, the police structure is further broken down into **municipal or district divisions**, which handle **community-level policing** and provide **specialized units** for tasks such as narcotics enforcement or emergency response.

In terms of size, the UAE police force is **robust in major population centers**, although complete national statistics are not made publicly available. The Abu Dhabi Police, for instance, employs around 12,500 frontline officers, and its total public safety workforce, including civil defense, ambulance, and border security staff, exceeds 36,000.[25] Similarly, the Dubai Police Force, which is known for its advanced technological infrastructure, employs more than 30,000 people in total, of whom approximately 17,500 are sworn officers.[26] Information on smaller emirates such as Ajman, Fujairah, and Umm Al Quwain is not comprehensively published, though each maintains its own local force under the same federal guidelines.

Determining whether the UAE's police forces are adequately staffed requires more than just numerical data; it also depends on workload, crime rates, and operational efficiency. What is clear, however, is that in places like Dubai and Abu Dhabi, the police are not only numerous but also **highly equipped with modern technology, including artificial intelligence, facial recognition, and autonomous patrol units.** For example, Dubai Police boasts an average emergency response time of 2 minutes and 24 seconds, which indicates a high level of readiness and resource allocation.[27]

Additionally, the staffing ratio in Abu Dhabi—where about one in every three public safety employees is a frontline officer—suggests a strong support structure in areas such as administration, logistics, and community services.

Although the numbers suggest that the police forces in major UAE cities like Dubai and Abu Dhabi are large and well-equipped, it's hard to say for sure if staffing is adequate across the whole country since the government doesn't share detailed data for the smaller emirates or provide national staffing benchmarks. Nevertheless, the reputation of the UAE police force is largely positive and widely considered professional, efficient, and well-organized.

25 https://academic.oup.com/policing/article/16/2/236/6563061

26 https://en.wikipedia.org/wiki/Dubai_Police_Force

27 https://www.dubaipolice.gov.ae/wps/portal/home/aboutus

Police Response

At the **federal level**, the Ministry of Interior (MOI) oversees the entire national policing framework. Its key functions include setting general law enforcement policy, coordinating between emirate police departments, managing federal-level investigations (especially in terrorism, cybercrime, and organized crime), overseeing border security, and operating federal prisons. The MOI also supervises national databases like criminal records and fingerprint registries, issues regulations on firearms and residency, and develops national strategies for emergency preparedness and civil defense.

At the **emirate level**, each of the seven emirates—such as Abu Dhabi, Dubai, Sharjah, and others—has its own police force. Their primary responsibilities include enforcing local laws and regulations, handling criminal investigations, regulating traffic, managing crime prevention programs, maintaining public order, and running local detention centers. Some emirate-level departments also have specialized units for narcotics, financial crimes, and VIP protection. For example, Dubai Police is known for its Cybercrime and Smart Services units, while Abu Dhabi Police has advanced counter-terror and forensic divisions.

At the **local or municipal level**, police stations and units within cities or neighborhoods carry out on-the-ground enforcement and community policing. They respond to emergencies, conduct patrols, handle minor criminal investigations, mediate disputes, enforce traffic and parking rules, and engage directly with the public. Local officers serve as the first point of contact for residents and tourists and often operate in multilingual, multicultural environments. Many emirates have also introduced **community policing programs** to build relationships with residents and encourage public cooperation in safety initiatives.

The UAE police face a unique set of challenges shaped by the country's rapid development, diverse population, and strict legal environment. One of the biggest challenges is **maintaining security and public trust** in a society where nearly 90% of the population are expatriates from widely varying cultural, religious, and legal backgrounds. This diversity can lead to misunderstandings of local laws—particularly those related to morality, public decency, and digital conduct—and puts pressure on police to balance firm enforcement with cultural sensitivity and communication. Missteps in handling such cases can attract international scrutiny and impact the country's global reputation.

Another significant challenge is **ensuring transparency and accountability** in policing and detention practices. While the UAE boasts low crime rates and high public safety rankings, international human rights organizations have raised concerns about the treatment of detainees, lack of independent oversight, and limited access to legal counsel in national security or political cases. There are also criticisms regarding the absence of press freedom and public reporting on internal police conduct, which limits civilian oversight and judicial transparency. Furthermore, as the country increasingly uses digital surveillance, artificial intelligence, and facial recognition, **questions about privacy rights and data protection** are becoming more pressing.

In response to both internal demands and global expectations, the UAE has initiated **a series of reforms** aimed at modernizing its police force and improving public service delivery. One of the most notable efforts is the introduction of **smart police stations**, especially in Dubai, which allow residents and visitors to report crimes, file complaints, and access services 24/7 without interacting with a human officer. These stations support multiple languages and are part of a broader initiative to create a "Police Without Policemen" model that relies heavily on automation and self-service.

Technology is a major pillar of ongoing reform. The UAE police, particularly in Dubai, are integrating artificial intelligence, predictive policing tools, and real-time surveillance systems to improve crime prevention and response times. These efforts are supported by training programs aimed at equipping officers with the skills to use new technologies effectively while maintaining ethical standards. In addition, there has been a noticeable push toward international cooperation and compliance with global law enforcement standards, particularly in areas such as counter-terrorism, human trafficking, and cybercrime.

There are also attempts to enhance community engagement and trust-building through public awareness campaigns, school programs, and increased access to multilingual support services. Some emirates have established special units focused on human rights, women's and children's safety, and the protection of vulnerable groups. These reforms indicate **a shift toward a more service-oriented model of policing**, where the focus extends beyond control to include public trust, communication, and modernization.

Police and Community Relations

The overall public perception of the police in the United Arab Emirates is **generally positive**, especially within the country's major cities such as Dubai and Abu Dhabi. The police are widely regarded as professional, disciplined, and efficient, contributing significantly to the UAE's reputation as one of the safest countries in the world. According to the Global Law and Order Report by Gallup, the UAE consistently ranks among the top countries where residents feel safe walking alone at night—an indicator that reflects public confidence in law enforcement.

Residents often highlight the police's quick response times, visible presence, and the advanced technologies they employ, such as AI surveillance, smart patrols, and automated stations. In Dubai, for instance, the police are not just viewed as enforcers but also as innovators, frequently promoting public safety through digital services, multilingual apps, and community outreach events. Their professionalism, combined with courteous interactions in many cases, helps build a generally favorable public image.

That said, perceptions vary somewhat among different population groups. Among expatriates, especially those from Western and Asian countries, views are mixed. While many appreciate the safety and order, others report feeling intimidated by the strictness of the laws and the potential for harsh penalties over relatively minor offenses—such as public displays of affection or posting content deemed offensive. Foreign residents unfamiliar with local norms may feel less secure in their interactions with police, especially when language barriers or cultural misunderstandings occur.

Critics, particularly from international human rights organizations, have raised **concerns about the lack of transparency in policing, the treatment of political detainees, and the limited availability of legal recourse** in certain cases. However, such issues are not typically visible in day-to-day policing or among the general population. Instead, they appear more in high-profile or sensitive cases involving national security.

Police Use of Force

The use of force by police in the United Arab Emirates is not widely viewed as a public issue in the way it is in some other countries. On a day-to-day basis, police interactions with the public are generally described as professional and orderly, especially in urban centers. Most residents, both local and expatriate, report feeling safe and do not typically witness violence or aggressive policing in public spaces. This is in part due to the UAE's strong emphasis on deterrence, advanced surveillance, and strict law enforcement, which collectively reduce the likelihood of confrontation.

However, this surface-level calm does not mean that the issue of police use of force is nonexistent. While there are **few publicly reported cases of excessive force in routine policing**, international human rights organizations have consistently raised **concerns about abuse in detention settings and during interrogations**—particularly in cases involving political dissidents, national security suspects, or those accused of cybercrimes or terrorism. According to reports by *Amnesty International* and *Human Rights Watch*, there have been instances where detainees were allegedly subjected to **incommunicado detention, torture, and coercive interrogations** to extract confessions. These claims typically come from cases involving Emiratis critical of the government, human rights defenders, or foreign nationals accused of serious offenses. Due to the opaque nature of the legal system in such cases, independent investigations and public records are limited, making it difficult to verify or assess patterns.

One notable case was that of **Ahmed Mansoor**, a prominent Emirati human rights activist who was arrested in 2017 and later sentenced to 10 years in prison. International observers, including the *UN Human Rights Office*, condemned his treatment, citing prolonged solitary confinement and lack of access to legal counsel as forms of cruel and degrading treatment (see Law of the Land True Story below).

In general, while the UAE police rarely display excessive force publicly or during routine law enforcement duties, the **lack of transparency, independent oversight, and press freedom** makes it difficult to assess the full scope of the problem. Most criticisms focus not on day-to-day patrols but rather on **closed-door practices** involving national security, political prisoners, or sensitive legal matters. Without a system of independent civilian review or regular public reporting on police conduct, concerns over accountability persist.

Law of the Land True Story[28]

Ahmed Mansoor is one of the most prominent human rights activists in the United Arab Emirates, internationally recognized for his advocacy on civil liberties, freedom of expression, and the rights of detainees in the Gulf region. A recipient of the Martin Ennals Award for Human Rights Defenders in 2015, Mansoor has been a rare voice of peaceful dissent in a country where criticism of the government is tightly restricted.

Mansoor was arrested on March 20, 2017, by UAE authorities and later sentenced in 2018 to 10 years in prison under cybercrime laws. The specific charges against him included "insulting the status and prestige of the UAE and its symbols," "publishing false information to harm the UAE's reputation abroad," and "using social media to spread sectarian and hate-inciting information." In reality, his "offenses" consisted of posting comments on Twitter and other platforms that criticized the

28 https://www.hrw.org/report/2021/01/27/persecution-ahmed-mansoor/how-united-arab-emirates-silenced-its-most-famous-human

UAE's human rights record and called for political reform, fair trials, and greater freedom of speech.

According to Amnesty International, Mansoor was arrested at his home in a midnight raid by a group of plainclothes officers, and his family was not informed of his whereabouts for weeks. He was held in solitary confinement for over a year, without access to a lawyer and with only extremely limited family contact. These conditions were described by UN experts as possibly amounting to torture or cruel, inhuman, and degrading treatment, in violation of international human rights law.

Reports suggest he was detained in a small isolation cell with no bed or access to reading material, and he was denied adequate medical care. In 2019, after his conditions were leaked to the media, he allegedly launched a hunger strike to protest his treatment. The UN Special Rapporteur on the situation of human rights defenders, along with other international bodies, repeatedly called on the UAE to release him or at least improve his prison conditions—but these appeals were ignored.

CHAPTER 16

HOW TO GET LEGAL HELP IN THE UAE

IN THIS CHAPTER

- Available Resources
- Legal Aid
- Foreign Embassies in the UAE

CHAPTER 16

HOW TO GET LEGAL HELP IN THE UAE

Available Resources

If you find yourself arrested while visiting the UAE, the first and most important step is to **contact your country's embassy or consulate** as soon as possible. The embassy can provide critical assistance such as verifying your well-being, informing your family, and guiding you through the local legal process. It is also helpful to identify which police station you have been taken to for any direct inquiries.

To find reliable legal representation, your embassy or consulate typically maintains a list of trusted local attorneys who have experience handling cases involving foreign nationals. They can recommend lawyers who are licensed to practice in the UAE and specialize in criminal law or other relevant areas. These attorney lists are often available on the consulate's official website and include contact details and information about the languages spoken by the lawyers. For example, the U.S. Embassy in Abu Dhabi provides a list of English-speaking attorneys specifically for American citizens, and other countries' consulates offer similar resources.

In case of emergencies, you can dial **999** for **police, ambulance, or fire services in the UAE.** Additionally, your embassy or consulate will have emergency contact numbers for after-hours support. The UAE Ministry of Interior also offers assistance and information related to legal and police matters and can be reached by phone or through their website.

While legal aid organizations for foreigners are limited, some **human rights or support groups** may offer guidance through embassy referrals. Having these contacts and resources in mind can be invaluable if you face legal trouble while visiting the UAE.

Legal Aid

Foreign visitors in the UAE are generally **not automatically eligible for government-funded legal aid** in the same way that citizens might be. Legal aid services in the UAE are limited and primarily aimed at residents or nationals who meet specific financial hardship criteria. However, foreign visitors who cannot afford legal representation can seek assistance through their embassy or consulate, which may provide guidance or recommend trusted lawyers. The process typically involves contacting your embassy first, who can help you understand your options and may facilitate access to legal support.

The criteria for any form of legal aid or assistance usually depend on financial need and the seriousness of the case. Since the UAE does not have a formal public defender system for foreigners, **access to free or subsidized legal aid is very limited,** and the burden is often on the individual to secure private counsel. Embassies may help connect visitors with lawyers willing to take cases on flexible payment terms or provide advice on navigating the legal system.

Legal aid in the UAE, when available, usually covers basic legal advice, help with documentation, and representation in court. It may include assistance with understanding charges, preparing a defense, and negotiating settlements. However, because formal legal aid programs for foreign visitors are scarce, the scope of help is often limited and dependent on the arrangements facilitated by diplomatic missions or private lawyers. Visitors are strongly encouraged to secure legal representation early and communicate regularly with their embassy to ensure proper support.

Foreign Embassies in the UAE

Foreign embassies and consulates in the UAE play an essential role in supporting their citizens who are living in or visiting the country. They provide a wide range of critical services, including emergency assistance during situations such as arrests, medical emergencies, or the loss of passports and important documents. Embassies serve as **a bridge between their home government and UAE authorities**, helping navigate the local legal system, offering guidance on laws and regulations, and facilitating communication with family or legal representatives abroad. Beyond crisis support, they also offer valuable information about safety, travel advisories, and cultural norms to help their citizens live and travel more securely in the UAE.

Most embassies and consulates are located in Abu Dhabi and Dubai, which are the UAE's two main international centers. **Abu Dhabi**, as the capital city, hosts the **majority of full embassies and diplomatic missions**, while **Dubai,** known as a global business and tourism hub, is home to **numerous consulates and honorary consulates.** This distribution ensures that foreign nationals can access consular services conveniently depending on their location in the country.

For U.S. citizens, the most prominent diplomatic missions in the UAE are the U.S. Embassy in Abu Dhabi and the U.S. Consulate General in Dubai. These offices offer a comprehensive range of services including visa and passport processing, emergency assistance, voter registration, and outreach programs for Americans living or traveling in the UAE. They also provide support for legal issues and can help connect citizens with local attorneys when needed.

A comprehensive list of embassies and consulates from other countries in the UAE can be accessed at **https://www.mofa.gov.ae/en/missions/foreign-missions-in-uae**.

CHAPTER 17

MEDICAL FACILITIES & HOSPITALS

IN THIS CHAPTER

- Overview
- Visitors' Access to Healthcare in the UAE
- UAE's Hospitals
- Insurance Guidance
- General Questions

CHAPTER 17

MEDICAL FACILITIES & HOSPITALS

Overview

The healthcare system in the United Arab Emirates is modern, well-funded, and **widely regarded as one of the best in the Middle East**. It features a combination of public and private facilities, with a strong emphasis on quality, innovation, and accessibility.

Healthcare affordability in the UAE depends largely on a person's residency status, insurance coverage, and whether care is sought in the public or private sector. For **UAE citizens** healthcare is **generally very affordable**, as the government provides extensive public health services either free of charge or at a nominal cost through facilities managed by local health authorities like SEHA in Abu Dhabi or the Dubai Health Authority. For **expatriates and foreign residents**, healthcare can be affordable **if they have insurance.** In Dubai and Abu Dhabi, employers are legally required to provide health insurance, which covers most basic medical needs. Out-of-pocket expenses such as copayments or non-covered services (like certain dental or cosmetic procedures) can still add up, but routine care remains reasonably priced for those with decent coverage.

Medical infrastructure is especially advanced in major cities, with internationally accredited hospitals, highly trained medical professionals, and state-of-the-art technology. The UAE has also positioned itself as a **hub for medical tourism**, attracting patients from around the world for elective procedures, specialized surgeries, and wellness services. In recent years, the country has heavily invested in digital health initiatives, including telemedicine and electronic health records, as part of its broader national development goals. While urban areas offer world-class healthcare, access in remote areas may be more limited, though mobile clinics and telehealth services are expanding to address this gap.

Visitors' Access to Healthcare in the UAE

Visitors to the UAE can access medical services relatively easily, but they must be prepared to pay for care either through **travel health insurance** or **out-of-pocket payments**. Unlike UAE citizens and residents who have access to public healthcare systems, tourists and short-term visitors are not eligible for subsidized treatment. As a result, they typically use **private hospitals and clinics**, which are widely available and often offer faster service, shorter wait times, and high-quality care. Many facilities are internationally accredited and equipped with modern technologies, attracting medical tourists as well as those seeking urgent or routine care while visiting.

Having valid **travel insurance is strongly recommended** and **often required** when applying for a tourist visa. Insurance policies usually cover emergency medical treatment, hospitalization, and repatriation, but visitors should read the fine print carefully to understand exclusions and coverage limits. In most cases, private hospitals will request payment upfront and issue a receipt or report for reimbursement through the visitor's insurance provider. Without insurance, healthcare services can be expensive. For example, a routine consultation at a private clinic may cost between **$80–$150 USD**, while emergency care or hospitalization can quickly reach several **thousand dollars** depending on the severity of the case.

Most private hospitals accept **major international insurance providers**, but it's a good idea for visitors to check in advance whether their insurance is recognized by a specific facility. Some hospitals also offer direct billing arrangements, while others may require patients to pay first and seek reimbursement later.

As for communication, **language barriers are rarely an issue** in UAE healthcare settings. English is the main language of communication in most private medical facilities, especially in major cities like **Dubai**, **Abu Dhabi**, and **Sharjah**. Medical staff are highly international, with doctors, nurses, and technicians from countries like the UK, India, the Philippines, and the US. In addition to Arabic and English, many providers also speak Hindi, Urdu, Tagalog, and other regional languages. Some hospitals also employ interpreters or offer multilingual support services to accommodate patients from diverse backgrounds. This makes it much easier for international visitors to describe symptoms, understand diagnoses, and navigate the healthcare process without confusion.

In summary, while healthcare access for visitors in the UAE is generally smooth and professional, it can be expensive without proper insurance. Fortunately, the country's widespread use of English in the medical sector, combined with high-quality facilities, ensures that most travelers receive prompt and effective care when needed.

UAE's Hospitals

The United Arab Emirates has built a robust and modern hospital network that supports both its growing population and its status as a hub for international healthcare. According to a UAE health report, the country had **172 hospitals** as of 2022, comprising **55 public (government) hospitals** and **117 private hospitals**. In total, the UAE had **5,369 healthcare facilities**—including clinics, specialized centers, and hospitals—at the end of 2020.[29] This infrastructure is supported by more than **90,000 healthcare professionals**, including doctors, nurses, and medical technicians, with that number continuing to rise due to active recruitment and investment in healthcare education.

Hospitals are heavily concentrated in the emirates of **Abu Dhabi**, **Dubai**, and **Sharjah**, which are home to the majority of the population and serve as the economic and medical centers of the country. These cities feature both advanced public facilities run by **the Abu Dhabi Health**

29 https://www.allocationassist.com/the-uae-healthcare-system

Services Company (**SEHA**) and **the Dubai Health Authority** (**DHA**), as well as cutting-edge private hospitals affiliated with international networks. Some of the best hospitals in the UAE include both public and private institutions. Among the public sector, **Sheikh Shakhbout Medical City** in Abu Dhabi stands out as one of the region's largest and most technologically advanced hospitals, and **Rashid Hospital** in Dubai is highly respected for its trauma and emergency care. In the private sector, leading names include **Cleveland Clinic Abu Dhabi**, a world-class facility affiliated with the U.S.-based Cleveland Clinic, known for cardiovascular and neurological specialties; **Mediclinic City Hospital**, part of the global Mediclinic Group; and the **American Hospital Dubai**, a Joint Commission International (JCI)-accredited facility offering care by North American and Western-trained physicians.

For international visitors, the UAE's private hospitals are especially accommodating. Many have dedicated international patient departments, multilingual staff, and agreements with global insurance providers to ensure smooth and accessible care. Dubai has made medical tourism a national priority, offering structured access to treatment through the **Dubai Health Experience** (**DXH**) initiative. There is an **American hospital in the UAE**: the **American Hospital Dubai** which one of the country's most prominent private institutions, delivering U.S.-standard healthcare to both residents and international patients.

Cumulatively, the UAE's hospital network reflects its commitment to becoming a global leader in healthcare by blending accessibility, high standards, and international partnerships.

Insurance Guidance

In terms of insurance, most private hospitals in both emirates accept **international** and **travel insurance plans.** Facilities such as Cleveland Clinic Abu Dhabi, Mediclinic, Burjeel, Aster, and American Hospital Dubai have **direct billing arrangements** with well-known global providers like Cigna, Bupa, Aetna, and Allianz. This means that insured patients may not have to pay upfront if their insurer is in-network. However, for travelers whose insurance isn't recognized or who lack insurance altogether, **out-of-pocket payment** is required before receiving treatment, except in emergencies.

Public hospitals such as those managed by SEHA in Abu Dhabi or the Dubai Health Authority (DHA) are primarily designated for UAE nationals and residents with local insurance. **Tourists and short-term visitors are generally not eligible for routine services at these public facilities.** Nonetheless, in a medical emergency, any hospital—public or private—is required to stabilize patients regardless of insurance status or ability to pay. After stabilization, patients may be transferred or discharged depending on their coverage and condition. Visitors are encouraged to carry valid travel insurance; in fact, under Dubai's five-year tourist visa scheme, **proof of medical coverage is mandatory.** Abu Dhabi offers short-term visitor insurance plans like ADNIC's HALA, which covers up to 150,000 AED (approximately $40,840 USD) for emergency treatment.

The cost of healthcare in the UAE varies depending on whether the patient visits a public or private facility. **For most foreigners, private hospitals are the default option and tend to be more expensive.** A general doctor's visit at a private clinic typically costs between 250 AED and 350 AED (about $68 USD to $95 USD), while a specialist consultation can range from 500 AED to 800 AED (about $136 USD to $218 USD). Emergency room visits without admission cost about 800 AED to 1,200 AED (about $218 USD to $327 USD). If hospitalization is necessary, the cost per day in a private facility is usually between 2,000 AED and 3,000 AED (about $545 USD to $817 USD). Procedures like childbirth or surgery can cost anywhere from 10,000 AED to over 30,000 AED (about $2,720 USD to $8,170 USD), depending on the complexity and hospital. Public healthcare facilities, when accessible, are subsidized and significantly cheaper—routine visits can cost as little as 20 AED to 50 AED (about $5.45 USD to $13.60 USD)—but are generally not open to tourists unless under emergency conditions.[30]

As the two most affluent and visited emirates, Dubai and Abu Dhabi share many healthcare standards but differ slightly in insurance

30 https://dxboffplan.com/the-cost-of-medical-services-in-abu-dhabi

regulations and systems. In Dubai, the **Dubai Health Authority** oversees the mandatory insurance scheme for residents, and the emirate has a broader mix of private insurers. Dubai also hosts **Dubai Healthcare City**, a dedicated medical free zone that caters to international patients with ease. Abu Dhabi's system is regulated by the **Department of Health** and relies heavily on the **Daman insurance network.** While both emirates maintain top-tier medical infrastructure, Abu Dhabi's public hospitals are generally more centralized under the SEHA umbrella, and Dubai has a denser concentration of private providers.

For foreign patients—whether tourists, temporary visitors, or newly arrived residents—the key is to maintain valid travel or private insurance, be prepared to pay out-of-pocket if needed, and understand that most care will be delivered through the private sector. Dubai and Abu Dhabi both offer a wide range of internationally accredited hospitals capable of delivering care comparable to Western standards, with staff who commonly speak English and other languages to accommodate the UAE's diverse population.

General Questions

1. ***What number do I call in* a medical emergency *in the UAE?*** In a **medical emergency** in the UAE, you should call **998**. This number connects you directly to ambulance services, which are operated by the local civil defense or health authorities. The service is available 24/7, and emergency responders are generally well-trained and equipped. Calls to 998 are free of charge, and English-speaking operators are available.

2. ***Will I be treated if I don't have insurance?*** **Yes.** You will be treated in a medical emergency in the UAE even if you don't have insurance. Hospitals—both public and private—are legally required to stabilize patients regardless of their insurance status or ability to pay. Once your condition is stabilized, however, you

may be transferred to another facility or discharged if you cannot cover ongoing costs. However, without insurance, you will be expected to pay out-of-pocket for all services beyond the initial emergency care.

3. ***Can I find English-speaking doctors in the UAE?*** **Yes.** You can easily find English-speaking doctors in the UAE. English is widely spoken throughout the country, especially in the health-care sector, which is staffed by a diverse, international workforce. In major cities like Dubai and Abu Dhabi, most doctors, nurses, and administrative staff are fluent in English, and many medical professionals have trained in the U.S., UK, Canada, or Australia.

4. ***Should I go to a public or private hospital?*** For most tourists, short-term visitors, and new expatriates, it's usually best to go to a **private hospital** in the UAE. Private hospitals are more accessible to non-residents, offer modern facilities, shorter wait times, and typically accept international insurance or upfront payment. Public hospitals mainly serve UAE nationals and residents with local insurance. They may limit services for visitors except in emergencies. That said, in a true emergency, all hospitals—public or private—are required to stabilize patients regardless of insurance status. Unless you have UAE government insurance or are specifically directed to a public facility, private hospitals are the more convenient and reliable option.

5. ***Do I need to pay upfront for medical treatment?*** **Yes.** In most cases, you will need to pay upfront for medical treatment in the UAE unless you have accepted insurance coverage. If your international or travel insurance is recognized by the hospital and includes direct billing, you may not need to pay at the time of service. However, many visitors—especially those without pre-approved insurance—are required to pay in full before receiving non-emergency care.

6. ***What if I need a prescription in the UAE?*** If you need a prescription in the UAE, you must first see a licensed doctor—either at a hospital or clinic—who will issue a prescription if necessary.

You cannot legally get prescription medications without consulting a doctor, even if it's a medication you use regularly at home. Once prescribed, you can fill the prescription at any licensed pharmacy, which are widely available and often open late, especially in cities like Dubai and Abu Dhabi.

7. ***Can I bring my medication to the UAE?*** **Yes.** You can bring your medication to the UAE, but there are important rules to follow. The country has strict regulations on controlled substances, and some common or over-the-counter medicines elsewhere may be restricted or banned. You should carry a valid prescription or a doctor's letter in English and bring only enough for personal use, usually about a 30-day supply. If your medication contains controlled substances like certain painkillers or ADHD treatments, you must get prior approval from the UAE Ministry of Health, which can be applied for online. Failure to follow these rules can result in confiscation or legal issues. It's best to check the UAE's list of restricted medications before traveling or consult your doctor or the UAE embassy.

8. ***What should I do in case of a medical emergency while traveling in the UAE?*** In case of a medical emergency while traveling in the UAE, you should immediately call the emergency number **998** to request an ambulance. Stay calm and clearly explain your location and the nature of the emergency. If possible, have someone nearby assist you with communication. Emergency responders will arrive quickly to provide on-site care and transport you to the nearest appropriate hospital.

CHAPTER 18

DRIVING IN THE UAE

IN THIS CHAPTER

- Overview
- Main Traffic Rules
- General Questions
- Law of the Land Hypothetical

CHAPTER 18

DRIVING IN THE UAE

Overview

Driving in the UAE offers a generally **smooth and efficient experience**, thanks to **well-maintained roads** and **modern infrastructure**. The country has invested heavily in its road network, resulting in wide highways, clear signage, and well-marked lanes. Major cities feature extensive multi-lane highways and well-planned urban roads, making driving relatively straightforward for both locals and visitors. However, traffic congestion can occur during peak hours, especially in Dubai, and some drivers may exhibit aggressive behavior, so caution is advised.

The road infrastructure is excellent, with frequent rest stops, service stations, and clear directional signs in both Arabic and English. Roads are regularly maintained, and **speed limits are strictly enforced** using numerous cameras and police patrols. Safety standards are generally high, with good lighting and clean, paved surfaces across urban and intercity routes.

Foreign drivers are required to carry a valid driving license recognized by the UAE, such as **an International Driving Permit** (**IDP**) alongside their home country license or a UAE driving license if they plan to stay long-term. Vehicle registration, insurance, and valid road tax documents must be in place. Comprehensive insurance coverage is strongly recommended for foreign drivers, as liability and collision costs can be high.

Unique driving customs include a generally fast-paced style, frequent use of the horn for communication, and courteous yielding in certain situations, though some aggressive driving and sudden lane changes are common. Flashing headlights are often used to signal giving way or warn of police presence ahead. Drivers should be aware of strict laws against reckless driving, speeding, and driving under the influence, which carry heavy fines and penalties.

Toll roads, known locally as **"Salik"** in Dubai and similar systems in other emirates, are common on major highways. These are electronic tolls with no toll booths; instead, vehicles are charged automatically via RFID tags or license plate recognition. Foreign drivers can rent or purchase a Salik tag from authorized outlets or online. Payment options typically include prepaid top-ups linked to the tag or automatic billing through linked accounts. It's important for visitors to ensure their vehicles have a functioning toll tag to avoid fines. Other emirates use similar systems with slightly different names and processes, but electronic tolling is standard across the UAE.

HELPFUL TIPS

Main Traffic Rules

- **Driving Side:** Vehicles drive on the **right-hand side** of the road, with overtaking on the left.
- **Speed Limits:** Speed limits vary by road type—typically **60–80 km/h (37–50 mph)** in urban areas and **100–140 km/h** (**62–87 mph**) on highways. Speed cameras are common, and exceeding limits can result in fines. Some roads allow a buffer of up to 10 km/h over the posted limit, but this varies by emirate.
- **Traffic Signals:** Standard traffic lights are used, with red-light violations strictly enforced. Roundabouts are common and usually operate on a **yield-to-the-left** system unless marked otherwise.

- **Seat Belts:** Seat belts are **mandatory for all passengers**, front and rear. Failing to wear one can lead to fines.
- **Alcohol: Zero-tolerance policy.** Driving under the influence of alcohol is strictly prohibited and punishable by jail time, heavy fines, and vehicle confiscation—even if only trace amounts are detected.
- **Mobile Devices:** Using a handheld phone while driving is **illegal** and subject to significant fines. Hands-free systems are permitted, but distractions are discouraged.
- **Toll Roads:** Electronic tolls operate in Dubai (Salik) and other emirates. Vehicles are charged automatically—**no cash or booths.** Visitors must ensure they have a registered Salik tag or rental cars equipped with one.
- **If Stopped by Police:** Remain calm and respectful. Provide your license, registration, insurance, and ID when asked. Do not exit the vehicle unless instructed. Arguing or filming officers is discouraged.
- **Road Safety Tips:** Always use indicators, check blind spots, and watch for sudden lane changes by others. Be extra cautious around large SUVs and trucks, which are common. Desert driving requires special preparation.

General Questions

1. ***Can I use my driver's license from my home country to drive in the UAE?*** **Yes.** You can use your driver's license from your home country to drive in the UAE, but it depends on your visa status and the country that issued your license. If you are a **tourist or short-term visitor**, you can drive legally in the UAE using your valid home country license **if it is from a recognized country** and accompanied by an **International Driving Permit** (**IDP**).

Some licenses from countries like the U.S., UK, Canada, and EU nations are often accepted on their own for rental cars, but it's safer to carry an IDP just in case. However, if you are a **UAE resident**, you must obtain a **UAE driver's license.** Residents can convert their existing licenses from certain approved countries without a driving test, while others must complete driving lessons and pass theory and road tests through a licensed driving institute. **Always check the current list of accepted countries with the UAE's Roads and Transport Authority (RTA) or the local traffic department.**

2. ***What is the age requirement for renting a car in the UAE?***
To rent a car in the UAE, you generally need to be at least **21 years old.** Some rental companies may have a higher minimum age—**25 or even 30**—for luxury or high-performance vehicles. Drivers under 25 may also face a "young driver surcharge." You'll need a valid driver's license (from a recognized country or with an International Driving Permit), passport, visa, and a credit card for the security deposit. While a few agencies may rent to 18–20-year-olds under strict conditions, this is rare and usually limited to basic vehicles with higher fees.

Law of the Land Hypothetical

HYPOTHETICAL: *Jason, a 24-year-old tourist from Canada, arrives in Dubai for a week-long vacation. He rents a car using his Canadian driver's license and drives to Abu Dhabi for a day trip. On the return trip, he's pulled over for speeding—he was going 130 km/h (81 mph) in a 100 km/h (62 mph) zone. He's issued a fine, but later wonders: since he's a tourist, does he have to pay the fine before leaving the UAE? What happens if he doesn't?*

ANSWER: **Yes.** *Even as a tourist, you are legally required to pay traffic fines incurred while driving in the UAE. Traffic violations are recorded under your vehicle rental and passport details, and unpaid fines can* *prevent you from leaving the country. In some cases, your rental company may withhold your deposit or charge your credit card for the fine. More seriously, if the fine is substantial or linked to a serious offense, it may trigger a* **travel ban** *or airport alert, delaying your departure. It's always best to settle any traffic fines promptly—either online through the Dubai Police or Abu Dhabi Police portals, or directly with your rental agency before returning the car.*

CHAPTER 19

NUDE BEACHES & CLOTHING-OPTIONAL RESORTS

IN THIS CHAPTER

- Overview
- Legality and Safety
- General Questions
- Law of the Land True Story

CHAPTER 19

NUDE BEACHES & CLOTHING-OPTIONAL RESORTS

Overview

Nudism is entirely incompatible with the cultural and legal norms of the United Arab Emirates. Rooted in conservative Islamic values, the UAE enforces **strict public decency laws that prohibit any form of public nudity or indecent exposure.** This includes not only complete nudity but also overly revealing clothing. What might be considered acceptable in parts of Europe or North America—such as topless sunbathing or nude saunas—is **illegal.**

There are **no legal or tolerated areas** where nudism is allowed, whether on beaches, in nature areas, or in private resorts. All public beaches and hotel-operated waterfronts follow national laws, which require modest swimwear. While many international hotels in Dubai or Abu Dhabi may be relaxed about dress codes within their premises, this **does not extend to nudity**, which remains off-limits even in adults-only or luxury settings. Moreover, hotel and resort staff are required to report any violations of public decency laws to authorities. The UAE also has a large population of conservative residents and foreign workers from similarly modest cultural backgrounds, which reinforces the societal expectation of appropriate dress and behavior.

Travelers should be aware that **even posting or sharing suggestive or semi-nude photos taken in the UAE on social media could attract**

legal trouble, especially if they are seen as disrespecting cultural norms. Respect for local values is not only a legal necessity but also an essential part of traveling responsibly in the region.

Legality and Safety

The UAE's Penal Code prohibits any form of public nudity or indecent exposure, including partial nudity or revealing clothing that may offend public morals. This applies not only in public spaces such as beaches, parks, or streets but also in private or semi-private areas if visible to others, such as hotel balconies or windows. Violating these laws can result in **arrest, hefty fines, imprisonment, and deportation**, regardless of whether the person is a resident or a visitor.

From a **safety** perspective, engaging in nudity in the UAE poses serious risks. Because the country enforces moral laws rigorously, individuals exposing themselves risk immediate police intervention and legal action. There is no social or legal tolerance for nudity, and anyone violating these norms may be subject to criminal charges without the protections or freedoms that might exist elsewhere. Even accidental or uninformed breaches can lead to detention or fines. Moreover, hotel staff or other guests may report such behavior, leading to swift consequences.

Unlike some countries where public nudity may be controversial but tolerated in certain contexts, in the UAE nudity is considered a serious offense and a threat to social order. Travelers should be aware that attempting to challenge these laws or asserting personal freedoms will not protect them from prosecution. Respecting local customs and dress codes is essential both for legal compliance and personal safety.

General Questions

1. ***Can I practice nudism inside a rented private Airbnb in the UAE without facing legal consequences?*** Even in a rented

private Airbnb in the UAE, practicing nudism carries legal risks if the nudity is visible to others outside the property, such as neighbors or passersby. UAE laws prohibit any form of public indecency, which can include nudity seen from outside your rental. While inside the property and completely out of public view, it is less likely to cause issues, but travelers should still exercise extreme caution. Authorities have acted on complaints from neighbors or others who observe such behavior, so privacy and discretion are crucial. Overall, nudism—even in private rentals like Airbnbs—is strongly discouraged to avoid potential legal trouble.

2. ***What should I wear when visiting a beach in the UAE to avoid any problems?*** When visiting a pool or beach in the UAE, it's important to wear modest and appropriate swimwear to respect local customs and avoid legal issues. For women, standard swimsuits such as one-piece suits or non-revealing bikinis are generally acceptable at hotel pools and private beaches, but overly revealing styles like thong bikinis or very sheer swimwear should be avoided. For men, swim trunks or shorts are appropriate, while speedos or excessively tight swimwear might attract unwanted attention. In public beaches, it's best to be more conservative, as these areas are often used by families and locals who expect modesty. Always follow any specific rules set by the hotel or beach authorities.

Law of the Land True Story[31]

In early 2025, a group of Russian tourists visiting the emirate of Sharjah were asked to leave a public beach and fined due to wearing swimsuits deemed too revealing by local authorities. The tourists were reportedly dressed in bikinis and other swimwear styles that are

31 https://eadaily.com/en/news/2025/04/19/in-the-uae-russian-tourists-were-kicked-off-the-beach-and-fined-because-of-swimsuits

common in many parts of the world but violated Sharjah's strict public decency regulations.

The incident occurred amid growing awareness that Sharjah maintains harsher restrictions on tourist attire, especially at public beaches and pools. According to reports, the tourists were confronted by local authorities or beach officials who informed them that their swimwear was not permitted under the emirate's laws. The tourists were then compelled to leave the beach and were fined as a penalty for violating the decency codes.

This case drew attention to the significant differences in enforcement between the emirates. While other popular tourist destinations in the UAE may tolerate bikinis and more revealing swimwear in private or designated areas, Sharjah maintains a zero-tolerance approach. The incident also highlighted how foreign visitors can unintentionally break local laws due to a lack of awareness about Sharjah's unique regulations.

Tour operators and local experts emphasize that visitors to Sharjah should adhere strictly to modest dress codes and avoid wearing bikinis or strapless swimsuits in public or semi-public places. This incident serves as a cautionary example illustrating the need for travelers to research local customs and legal expectations before visiting different parts of the UAE.

CHAPTER 20

UNUSUAL LAWS

IN THIS CHAPTER

- Overview
- UAE's Unusual Laws
- General Questions
- Law of the Land True Story

CHAPTER 20

UNUSUAL LAWS

Overview

Unusual laws can be fascinating glimpses into a culture's values and history. While most people are aware of common legal restrictions, it's often the strange and quirky laws that capture our attention. These regulations can range from the amusing to the absurd, reflecting the unique circumstances and traditions of a place. Whether they arise from historical events, societal norms, or simply peculiar local customs, unusual laws can provide insight into the quirks of human behavior and governance.

HELPFUL TIPS

UAE's Unusual Laws

The United Arab Emirates is a modern, fast-developing country that welcomes millions of visitors each year—but beneath its gleaming skyline and luxury resorts lies a legal system rooted in Islamic values and local traditions. Many travelers are surprised to learn that everyday behaviors considered normal elsewhere can be illegal in the UAE. Here are some of the country's more unusual or lesser-known laws, along with the penalties for breaking them, to help visitors stay informed, respectful, and out of trouble during their stay:

Swearing—Even Online

Using profane language in person, in writing, or online (including WhatsApp or social media) is a criminal offense. This includes insults, rude gestures (like flipping the finger), and even emojis that could be interpreted as offensive. Penalties can include **fines up to 250,000 AED** (about **$68,000 USD**) and **jail time or deportation.**

Public Displays of Affection

Kissing, hugging, or even holding hands in public—particularly between unmarried couples—can result in fines, arrest, or deportation. While married couples holding hands are generally tolerated in places like Dubai, more conservative emirates like Sharjah are stricter.

Taking Photos Without Permission

Photographing people—especially women—or government buildings, airports, or accident scenes without consent is prohibited and can lead to **fines, jail time, or confiscation of your device.** This law is strictly enforced, even for tourists.

Dancing in Public

Public dancing and loud music in non-designated areas (like beaches or streets) are considered acts of public disturbance. This includes impromptu celebrations or music gatherings. Violators may be fined or detained.

Possession of Poppy Seeds

While poppy seeds are common in many countries' baked goods, they are banned in the UAE as they are considered a narcotic. Even trace amounts found in luggage can lead to **arrest or imprisonment**.

Eating or Drinking on Public Transport

It's illegal to eat or drink on public transportation in cities like Dubai. Violators may be fined **100 AED** (about **$27 USD**).

Sharing Hotel Rooms if Unmarried

Technically, it's against the law for unmarried couples to share a hotel room. While this rule has relaxed somewhat—especially in Dubai—it's still enforced in more conservative areas and remains on the books.

General Questions

1. ***Can using certain emojis or gestures on social media lead to legal consequences in the UAE?*** **Yes.** In the UAE, using certain emojis, gestures, or language on social media can indeed lead to legal consequences. The country's laws prohibit offensive or insulting behavior online, which includes sending rude messages, hateful comments, or even emojis that could be interpreted as offensive or disrespectful. This is taken very seriously under the UAE's cybercrime laws, and violations can result in hefty fines, imprisonment, and even deportation for foreigners. So, travelers and residents alike should be cautious about their online behavior and avoid sharing anything that might be deemed inappropriate or offensive under local standards.

2. ***How strictly are unusual laws and penalties enforced in the UAE, especially for tourists unfamiliar with local customs?*** In the UAE, laws—especially those related to public decency, behavior, and morality—are enforced **quite strictly**, regardless of whether someone is a local resident or a tourist. Authorities take violations seriously to uphold cultural values and maintain public order. Tourists unfamiliar with local customs have faced

fines, detention, or even deportation for offenses that might seem minor elsewhere, such as inappropriate dress, public displays of affection, or offensive language. While enforcement can vary somewhat by emirate and situation, it's safest for visitors to assume that the laws will be applied firmly and to take care to respect local rules to avoid legal trouble.

Law of the Land True Story[32]

Craig Ballentine, a 33-year-old autism support worker from Cookstown, Northern Ireland, was arrested in October 2024 upon his arrival at Abu Dhabi airport. The arrest stemmed from a negative Google review he had posted about a dog grooming salon in Dubai, where he had previously worked. In the review, he detailed issues related to his treatment after taking medical leave for fibromyalgia. Despite providing a doctor's certificate, the salon had reported him as "absconded," leading to a travel ban that prevented him from leaving the UAE.

Upon his return to the UAE for a short holiday, Ballentine was detained and charged with slander under the UAE's strict cybercrime laws, which prohibit online criticism. He was transferred from Abu Dhabi to Dubai to await the outcome of his case. In December 2024, after two months in detention, Ballentine was unexpectedly released and allowed to return home just before Christmas. He had paid a fine and served a one-month social media ban. However, due to an appeal from his former employer, he faced the possibility of returning to Dubai for further court hearings in early 2025.

This case has highlighted concerns about the UAE's cybercrime laws and their potential misuse, particularly against foreigners. Advocacy groups like Detained in Dubai have criticized the legislation for enabling extortion and for its severe impact on individuals who may not

32 https://www.thetimes.com/uk/society/article/briton-faces-jail-in-dubai-after-criticising-ex-boss-on-google-wrl7zjjd7

be aware of the stringent regulations. Ballentine's experience underscores the importance for travelers to be cautious about their online activity and to understand the legal implications of their actions in the UAE.

CHAPTER 21

TRAVELING SAFELY

IN THIS CHAPTER

- Ladies Traveling Solo
- Traveling as a Family
- Do's and Don'ts While in the UAE

CHAPTER 21
TRAVELING SAFELY

Ladies Traveling Solo

The United Arab Emirates (UAE) enjoys a strong reputation as one of the safest countries in the Middle East, and in many respects, the world. With extremely low crime rates and rigorous law enforcement, it is widely considered a **secure destination for both residents and tourists.** Violent crime is rare, and petty crimes such as theft or scams are infrequent, especially in major urban centers. The country's heavy use of surveillance cameras and visible police presence contribute to this sense of security.

For solo travelers—and especially solo female travelers—the UAE is generally a very safe destination. Women walking alone in public areas, using public transportation, or exploring tourist attractions usually encounter no issues. In major cities, it is common to see women traveling alone for business or leisure, and this is not regarded as unusual or inappropriate. Female tourists are treated with respect in most settings, and many report feeling safer in the UAE than in cities in Europe or North America.

However, attitudes toward solo women can **vary somewhat by location.** In more conservative emirates like Sharjah, Umm Al Quwain, or Ras Al Khaimah, cultural expectations are stricter, and solo female travelers may draw more attention, especially if they are dressed in revealing or Western-style clothing. Although this attention is rarely aggressive, dressing modestly—covering shoulders, cleavage, and knees—helps women avoid unwanted stares or misunderstandings. Wearing more conservative attire in public spaces such as souks, religious sites, and public transport is both respectful and practical.

Social customs also discourage flirtatious or physical interaction between unrelated men and women in public, which can work in favor of solo female travelers by reducing unwanted advances. Harassment is rare and taken seriously by authorities. Women who experience inappropriate behavior can report it to police with confidence that it will be investigated. Legal protections for women are robust in this area, and even verbal harassment can lead to arrest or deportation for offenders.

There are no officially "dangerous" neighborhoods, but industrial areas or poorly lit outskirts are best avoided after dark, simply due to lack of pedestrian traffic and services. In cities like Dubai and Abu Dhabi, central areas, malls, hotels, beaches, and major attractions are generally safe at all hours.

Traveling as a Family

The United Arab Emirates (UAE) is widely considered a safe, convenient, and **family-friendly destination**. With modern infrastructure, high public safety standards, and a wealth of child-friendly attractions, it offers a comfortable experience for families traveling with children. Cities like Dubai and Abu Dhabi, in particular, are designed to accommodate the needs of international tourists and provide easy access to healthcare, clean public spaces, and entertainment options tailored for all ages.

Health precautions for families primarily center around the country's intense heat, especially during the summer when temperatures can exceed 110°F (43°C). It's important to keep children well-hydrated, avoid prolonged sun exposure during midday hours, and apply sunscreen regularly. Fortunately, most public spaces and accommodations are air-conditioned. Bottled water is widely available and safe to drink, and the food safety standards in hotels and restaurants are high. However, it's still wise to avoid street food in more rural or unfamiliar areas when traveling with small children. Routine vaccinations are generally sufficient for entry, but families may want to consult a pediatrician before travel to ensure all immunizations are up to date.

Family accommodations in the UAE are plentiful and well-equipped. Most international hotel chains and resorts offer interconnected rooms, suites with kitchenettes, and kid-friendly amenities such as cribs, high chairs, and childproofed spaces. Many resorts also feature kids' clubs, splash zones, and babysitting services. Large attractions **like Motiongate Dubai, Ferrari World Abu Dhabi,** and **Yas Waterworld** cater specifically to children, and even shopping malls include indoor playgrounds, aquariums, cinemas, and entertainment centers.

In terms of safety, the UAE is extremely secure, with a very low crime rate and widespread use of surveillance in public places. Child abductions or crimes involving minors are extremely rare. Nonetheless, parents should remain attentive in busy areas like markets or festivals. Public malls and entertainment venues typically have staff trained to handle lost children, and most beaches and hotel pools have lifeguards on duty. That said, water safety remains important, and children should not be left unattended near pools or in the ocean.

Families traveling in the UAE should also be aware of cultural expectations. Children should be dressed modestly in public, and although affection between parents and children is fine, public displays should remain respectful, particularly in more conservative emirates. When using taxis or ride-hailing services, bringing a child safety seat is advisable, as not all vehicles are equipped with them by default—though they are legally required for children under age four.

With thoughtful planning, cultural awareness, and attention to heat and hydration, the UAE offers a secure and enjoyable environment for families. From luxury resorts and world-class theme parks to strong public safety and modern healthcare, the country stands out as a top-tier destination for those traveling with children.

Do's and Don'ts While in the UAE

When visiting the United Arab Emirates, understanding local customs, laws, and cultural expectations is essential to ensure a respectful and trouble-free experience. The UAE is modern and welcoming but remains rooted in Islamic traditions that influence daily life, especially in public behavior. Here are key do's and don'ts to keep in mind.

DO:

- **Dress modestly** in public spaces, especially in mosques, traditional markets, and more conservative emirates like Sharjah. Women should cover shoulders and knees, and men should avoid wearing sleeveless shirts.
- **Respect religious practices**, particularly during the holy month of Ramadan. Avoid eating, drinking, or smoking in public during daylight hours, and be mindful of religious sensitivities.
- **Use your right hand** for greeting, eating, and handing items, as the left hand is traditionally considered unclean.
- **Ask permission before photographing people**, especially Emirati women and families. Always be respectful when taking photos in religious or government buildings.
- **Follow local laws** closely. The UAE has zero tolerance for drugs, strict decency laws, and detailed regulations that may differ significantly from your home country.
- **Be polite and courteous.** Public behavior is expected to be respectful and non-confrontational at all times.
- **Use official taxis or apps** like Uber and Careem for reliable transport, and buckle up—seat belts are mandatory.

DON'T:

- **Don't engage in public displays of affection** like kissing or hugging, which can be considered offensive or even illegal.
- **Don't use rude gestures or curse** in public; such actions can lead to fines, arrest, or deportation.
- **Don't engage in drunken behavior** in public spaces. Alcohol is allowed in licensed venues, but public intoxication is illegal and taken seriously.
- **Don't bring prohibited items**, such as pork products, certain medications, or pornographic material. Even over-the-counter medications from your home country may be banned, so check before you travel.
- **Don't speak disrespectfully about religion, the royal family, or the government**, in person or online—this can lead to criminal charges.
- **Don't cohabit or share a hotel room with a romantic partner** if you are unmarried. While enforcement is more relaxed in tourist areas, the law still exists, especially in more conservative parts of the country.

Engaging with local culture in the United Arab Emirates can be a deeply rewarding part of your visit, but it's important to do so with awareness and respect. Emiratis are known for their hospitality, but they also place great value on tradition, modesty, and etiquette. Whether you're speaking with locals, visiting heritage sites, or attending a cultural event, showing cultural sensitivity goes a long way.

Start by greeting people politely. A simple "**As-salamu alaykum**" (peace be upon you) is always appreciated, especially in more traditional settings. When addressing Emiratis, use formal titles like "**Sheikh**" or "**Sheikha**" when appropriate, and always address elders with added respect. Handshakes are common among men, but men should wait for a woman to offer her hand first—if she doesn't, a nod or verbal greeting is more appropriate.

Modesty in both behavior and clothing is key. Even in cosmopolitan cities like Dubai or Abu Dhabi, dressing conservatively shows respect for the culture. This is especially important when visiting mosques, cultural centers, or rural areas. At religious or national events, observe quietly, ask questions respectfully, and avoid taking photos unless it's clearly permitted.

Hospitality is a major part of Emirati culture. If invited into someone's home, remove your shoes before entering, accept refreshments with your right hand, and avoid showing the soles of your feet. Complimenting something in the home may result in the host offering it to you—so be cautious not to express admiration unless you truly mean it.

Engaging with the local culture also means being mindful of religious customs. Avoid interrupting prayer times, and if you're present when the call to prayer is heard, pause momentarily out of respect. During Ramadan, be particularly sensitive—don't eat, drink, or smoke in public during daylight hours, and be extra courteous in your interactions.

While Emiratis are generally private and family-oriented, many are happy to answer respectful questions about their traditions, clothing, and way of life—especially in designated cultural spaces like the Sheikh Mohammed Centre for Cultural Understanding in Dubai or Qasr Al Hosn in Abu Dhabi.

Ultimately, approaching the local culture with humility, curiosity, and mindfulness will lead to more authentic and respectful connections—and likely leave you with a much deeper appreciation of life in the UAE.

CHAPTER 22

TOURIST TAXATION

IN THIS CHAPTER

- Overview
- Tourist Taxes in the UAE
- Law of the Land Hypothetical

CHAPTER 22

TOURIST TAXATION

Overview

Tourism plays a vital role in the UAE's broader economic framework, especially as the country diversifies away from oil dependency. Over the past two decades, the UAE—particularly Dubai and Abu Dhabi—has invested heavily in becoming a **global hub for leisure, business, and luxury travel.** Iconic attractions like the **Burj Khalifa, Louvre Abu Dhabi, Yas Island theme parks, desert resorts,** and **world-class shopping festivals** have made the country a premier destination. In fact, tourism contributed approximately 12% to the UAE's GDP in recent years, with goals to increase that figure significantly through the government's long-term vision, such as the UAE Tourism Strategy 2031.[33]

Dubai, for example, consistently ranks **among the world's most visited cities** and serves as a major transit point between Europe, Asia, and Africa. Abu Dhabi has positioned itself as a cultural capital, while other emirates like Ras Al Khaimah are promoting eco-tourism and adventure travel. The tourism sector also supports other key industries such as real estate, hospitality, retail, and aviation.

Tourists in the UAE are required to pay certain taxes and fees not only to generate government revenue but also to fund the continued

33 https://wttc.org/news/international-traveller-spend-uae-to-reach-a-record-aed-228bn

development and maintenance of the country's world-class tourism infrastructure. These charges typically include a **tourism dirham** (a per-night hotel fee), **municipality taxes** on hotel and restaurant bills (usually around 5% to 10%), and a **value-added tax (VAT)** of 5% on goods and services. These fees help offset the cost of public services that support tourism—such as security, transportation, and cultural preservation—while allowing the UAE to maintain its competitive position as a top global destination.

In essence, tourism is not just a side attraction in the UAE; it is a central pillar of its economic future, and the associated taxes are one way the government sustains the high quality of experience that international visitors have come to expect.

Tourist Taxes in the UAE

Tourist taxes in the UAE are an important aspect of the country's strategy to fund and maintain its world-class tourism infrastructure and services. These taxes are generally included in the cost of accommodations, dining, and entertainment, so tourists often pay them automatically without needing to navigate a complex tax system.

One of the main types of tourist taxes is the **Tourism Dirham**, which is primarily applied in Dubai. This is a fixed nightly fee charged per hotel room, and the amount varies depending on the hotel's star rating or classification. The fees range from 7 AED to 20 AED per night, which converts to approximately $1.90 to $5.45 USD. This fee helps Dubai invest in developing and maintaining its hospitality and tourism services, ensuring visitors have a high-quality experience.

In addition to the Tourism Dirham, there is a **municipality tax** applied across the UAE, which typically appears on hotel bills, restaurant checks, and entertainment venues. This tax usually ranges from **5% to 10%** of the total bill. For example, in Abu Dhabi, visitors pay a 6% tourism fee alongside a 4% municipality fee on hotel bills, plus a fixed charge of 15 AED (about $4.08 USD) per room per night. These taxes support local municipal services, including infrastructure maintenance, security, and sanitation, all of which contribute to a safe and pleasant environment for tourists.

Hotels and restaurants often add a **service charge** of around **10%**, which can be combined with municipality taxes on final invoices. Additionally, the UAE has implemented a **value-added tax (VAT)** of **5%**, which applies broadly to goods and services, including those used by tourists such as shopping, dining, car rentals, and tours. This VAT is a general tax that supports government revenue but also helps fund public services utilized by residents and visitors alike.

The payment process for these taxes is seamless for tourists because they are **automatically included in bills for accommodation, meals, and entertainment.** Tourists typically do not need to take any extra steps to pay these taxes or file any documentation. However, it is a good practice for travelers to review their bills carefully to understand the breakdown of charges, especially in places like Dubai where multiple fees—such as the Tourism Dirham, municipality tax, service charge, and VAT—may appear separately.

One important point for tourists is that while **VAT can sometimes be reclaimed** on eligible purchases through VAT refund schemes at airports, the other tourism-related taxes such as the Tourism Dirham and municipality fees are **not refundable**. Furthermore, these taxes and fees can vary slightly depending on the emirate. For instance, Sharjah applies different municipality rates compared to Dubai or Abu Dhabi, and the Tourism Dirham is specific to Dubai. Travelers should be aware of these regional differences to avoid surprises.

Overall, these tourist taxes play a key role in sustaining the UAE's investment in its tourism sector, helping to maintain cleanliness, safety, and high standards of service that contribute to the country's reputation as a top global destination. While these taxes add a modest amount to travel costs, they are part of the reason why visitors experience such well-developed infrastructure and amenities throughout the UAE.

Law of the Land Hypothetical

HYPOTHETICAL: *Liam, a 34-year-old tourist from Australia, books a hotel stay in Abu Dhabi through an online travel site. Upon checking out, he notices a municipality tax and service charge added to his bill that were not mentioned during booking. Liam questions the hotel staff about whether these extra fees are mandatory and if he can refuse to pay them since they weren't clearly disclosed upfront. Is Liam legally required to pay these additional taxes and fees in Abu Dhabi, and what could happen if he refuses?*

ANSWER: **Yes.** *Liam is legally required to pay the additional municipality tax and service charges added to his hotel bill in Abu Dhabi. These fees are mandated by the government and are standard across hotels in the UAE, even if they were not clearly disclosed during the online booking process. Hotels collect these charges on behalf of the authorities and include them in the final invoice. If Liam refuses to pay these fees, the hotel can legally withhold services such as releasing his room or providing a checkout until payment is made. In some cases, refusal to pay may lead to involvement from local authorities, potential fines, or difficulties securing future accommodations. It is important for tourists to understand that these taxes and fees are part of the overall cost of hospitality services in the UAE and cannot be waived or negotiated. To avoid surprises, travelers should confirm all applicable taxes and fees before finalizing bookings.*

CHAPTER 23

LONG-TERM STAYS

IN THIS CHAPTER

- Overview
- Long-Term Visas and Application Requirements
- General Questions
- Law of the Land True Story
- Takeaways

CHAPTER 23
LONG-TERM STAYS

Overview

The UAE is a highly desirable destination for long-term stays due to a **unique combination of financial advantages, career prospects, quality of life,** and **cultural diversity.** One of the most appealing aspects is the **absence of personal income tax**, allowing residents to retain more of their earnings and significantly increase their savings potential. This, coupled with a thriving job market—especially in sectors **like finance, real estate, technology, healthcare,** and **tourism**—makes the UAE an attractive place for skilled professionals from around the world.

Life in the UAE offers a remarkably high standard of living. Residents enjoy access to modern infrastructure, luxury housing, top-tier shopping, world-class dining, and advanced medical facilities. The cities of Dubai and Abu Dhabi, in particular, are known for their architectural innovation and vibrant social scenes. Safety is another major draw; the UAE consistently ranks **among the safest countries globally**, with low crime rates and a reputation for strict law enforcement and political stability. Furthermore, the country's infrastructure is modern and efficient, with clean and well-maintained roads, high-speed internet, reliable utilities, and excellent public transportation systems such as the Dubai Metro. It is also home to some of the busiest and most well-connected airports in the world, making international travel easy and convenient.

Culturally, the UAE is **incredibly diverse and welcoming.** Nearly 90% of the population consists of expatriates from over 200 nationalities, and **English is widely spoken**, making it easy for newcomers to adjust. The government promotes tolerance and inclusivity, allowing various cultures and religions to coexist peacefully. International schools, community events, and places of worship for many faiths reflect the country's openness.

The UAE's strategic location between Europe, Asia, and Africa further adds to its appeal. It serves as a **convenient base for global business and travel**, with many major cities only a short flight away. Families also find the UAE appealing thanks to its abundance of international schools, child-friendly amenities, and safe neighborhoods. Additionally, **recent visa reforms** have made it even more attractive to stay long-term. Programs like the Golden Visa and Green Visa offer five- and ten-year renewable residency options for investors, entrepreneurs, highly skilled professionals, and freelancers, without requiring citizenship or local sponsorship. These reforms give residents a greater sense of permanence and stability.

Altogether, the UAE offers an exceptional blend of economic opportunity, cosmopolitan living, and long-term security, making it one of the most sought-after destinations for expatriates worldwide.

Long-Term Visas and Application Requirements

The United Arab Emirates offers several long-term residency visa options designed to attract investors, skilled professionals, entrepreneurs, retirees, and remote workers. These visas vary in duration and eligibility, but all aim to position the UAE as a global hub for talent and investment:

The **Golden Visa** is one of the most prestigious residency options. It grants a 5- or 10-year renewable residency. Investors who commit at least 2,000,000 AED (approximately $545,000 USD) in real estate or approved investment funds are eligible. Entrepreneurs who own a business worth 500,000 AED (about $136,000 USD) or more, especially if supported by incubators like HUB71 or AREA 2071, can apply. Highly skilled professionals such as doctors, engineers, and executives earning 50,000 AED ($13,600 USD) or more monthly also qualify. Outstanding students with GPAs of 3.8 or above, PhD holders, and individuals recognized for scientific or artistic achievements are eligible too. The Golden Visa allows holders to sponsor family members including spouses, children of any age, parents, and domestic workers. Unlike standard visas, it does not require employer sponsorship or a minimum stay, allowing holders to live abroad without losing residency.

The **Green Visa** offers a five-year renewable residency for skilled workers, freelancers, and investors. Skilled workers need a bachelor's degree and a monthly salary of at least 15,000 AED (about $4,100 USD). Freelancers and self-employed applicants must show proof of income totaling 360,000 AED (around $98,000 USD) over the past two years or demonstrate financial solvency. Investors and partners must prove involvement in a UAE-based business with a capital investment of at least 1,000,000 AED ($272,000 USD). This visa does not require employer sponsorship, includes generous grace periods, and allows sponsoring first-degree family members. The processing fee averages around 3,000 AED ($820 USD), with approval times typically between two and four weeks.

The **Blue Residency Visa**, newly introduced, is a 10-year visa targeting professionals in environmental sustainability and climate-related fields. It aims to attract top talent supporting the UAE's climate action goals. Applicants should demonstrate significant experience or recognized contributions in sustainability roles. Specific financial requirements and processing details are still being finalized.

The **Retirement Visa** is for UAE residents aged 55 or older meeting financial criteria such as owning property worth 1,000,000 AED ($272,000 USD) or having savings of the same amount or earning a monthly income or pension of 15,000 AED ($4,100 USD). Valid health insurance and proof of accommodation are required. The visa is valid for five years and renewable, offering retirees a way to live comfortably in the UAE post-career.

The **Remote Work or Digital Nomad Visa** allows foreign professionals to reside in the UAE for up to one year while working remotely for companies outside the UAE. Applicants must provide proof of employment or freelance contracts, a minimum monthly income of 3,500 USD (roughly $13,000 AED), valid health insurance, and a passport valid for at least six months. This visa supports the growing remote work trend and permits holders to bring immediate family members.

Applying for long-term visas in the UAE involves a structured process that begins with preparing the necessary documents such as a valid passport with at least six months of validity, passport photos, proof of financial means or investment, a medical fitness certificate from a UAE-approved health center, health insurance, and a clean criminal record certificate from your home country. Depending on the visa type, additional documentation may be required, such as proof of property ownership, business licenses, or academic credentials.

The application is submitted **online through official government portals**. For Dubai, this is the **General Directorate of Residency and Foreigners Affairs** (**GDRFA**), while the other emirates use the **Federal Authority for Identity, Citizenship, Customs and Port Security** (**ICP**) **Smart Services portal.** Some applicants may use authorized typing centers to assist with the paperwork.

Once the application is submitted, visa fees must be paid. These **fees vary by visa type**, typically ranging from around 1,300 AED (about $350 USD) for remote work visas up to approximately 13,000 AED (around $3,540 USD) for Golden Visas. After the initial approval, applicants are required to undergo **medical testing,** which includes blood tests and chest X-rays at approved health centers, followed by **biometric registration**, such as fingerprints and photographs.

After completing these steps, an **entry permit** is issued, allowing the applicant to enter the UAE if applying from abroad. Upon arrival or within the UAE (if converting a visit visa), applicants finalize the residency visa process by completing paperwork and registering for an **Emirates ID.** The residency visa is then issued and linked to the passport electronically or stamped, depending on the process.

Processing times vary depending on the visa type. **Golden Visas** generally take between **one to eight weeks**, with real estate investors often receiving faster approvals within one to two weeks, while professionals and students may experience longer processing due to additional background checks. **Green Visas** usually take around **two to four weeks** for approval. **Remote work visas** are among the quickest, typically processed within **one to two weeks. Retirement visas** generally take **three to four weeks** after all required documents are submitted.

Delays can occur if further documentation is requested or verifications take longer, so it is advisable to **apply well ahead** of the intended move date to the UAE.

General Questions

1. ***If I want to stay in the UAE for long-term and work, should I apply for a work permit* before *arriving in the UAE?*** **Yes.** If you plan to live and work long-term in the UAE, you generally need to secure a work permit or a work-based residency visa **before arriving**. Employers in the UAE usually sponsor your work permit and residency visa, so having a valid job offer is essential before you apply. The employer initiates the process by obtaining a work permit (also called a labor card), after which you can apply for a residency visa linked to that permit. Entering the UAE on a tourist visa and then trying to convert it to a work visa is possible but can be complicated, time-consuming, and sometimes discouraged by authorities. It's best to have your work permit and residency visa arranged beforehand to ensure a smooth and legal transition to long-term work and residence in the country.

2. ***I am American. Can I retire to the UAE?*** **Yes.** As an American, you can retire to the UAE. The country offers a specific **Retirement Visa** program designed for residents aged 55 and

older who meet certain financial criteria. The Retirement Visa is usually issued for five years and is renewable, allowing retirees to live comfortably in the UAE with access to its modern amenities, healthcare, and lifestyle benefits. This visa provides a legal path for Americans and other nationals who want to enjoy the UAE's tax advantages, safety, and high quality of life during their retirement years.

Law of the Land True Story[34]

The UAE's announcement of visa overstay fine waivers for Iranian nationals is a significant humanitarian response to the ongoing Israel–Iran conflict, which has left many travelers and residents stranded. Under normal circumstances, anyone who overstays their visa in the UAE is subject to daily fines that can quickly add up—sometimes totaling thousands of dirhams. However, in this case, the UAE government has chosen to suspend all such penalties for Iranians currently within the country, regardless of how long they've overstayed or what type of visa they originally held.

This policy, effective from June 17, 2025, and running through December 31, 2025, is aimed specifically at individuals who have been unable to leave due to travel disruptions, canceled flights, or safety concerns related to the conflict. The waiver allows them to stay in the UAE legally without the fear of accumulating or having to pay steep fines, and it gives them time to either regularize their immigration status or make safe travel plans once conditions improve.

The move highlights the UAE's ongoing efforts to balance strict immigration enforcement with compassion during times of crisis. It also helps relieve the financial burden on those caught in an international emergency, many of whom may be separated from family or dealing

34 https://timesofindia.indiatimes.com/world/middle-east/uae-waives-overstay-fines-for-iranians-stranded-amid-israel-iran-conflict-valid-until-end-of-2025/articleshow/121917640.cms

with uncertainty about when it will be safe to return home. At this time, the waiver applies only to Iranian nationals, and no similar broad relief has been announced for other nationalities. Those eligible are encouraged to contact the UAE's Federal Authority for Identity, Citizenship, Customs and Port Security (ICP) for details on how to benefit from the exemption, particularly if they need to renew their residency or arrange legal departure.

Takeaways

The UAE appeals to long-term residents thanks to **zero personal income tax**, high salaries in sectors like tech and finance, world-class infrastructure, and a cosmopolitan, safe lifestyle. Dubai and Abu Dhabi offer luxury, safety, and connectivity that attract global professionals and families alike.

There are several long-term residency visas, including the **Golden Visa** (5–10 years for investors, top professionals, students), **Green Visa** (5 years for skilled workers and freelancers), **Retirement Visa** (5 years for those 55+ with financial means), **Remote Work Visa** (1 year for digital nomads), and **Blue Residency Visa** (10 years for sustainability professionals). Each has clear financial, professional, or investment requirements.

- Applications must be submitted online through government portals like the GDRFA or ICP, along with medical exams and biometric data. Costs range from 1,300 AED (about $350 USD) to 13,000 AED (around $3,540 USD), depending on the visa type. Processing typically takes 1–8 weeks depending on complexity.
- Americans planning to work long-term in the UAE must secure a work permit through employer sponsorship before arrival. Americans aged 55 and above can also retire in the UAE using a

renewable Retirement Visa if they meet financial thresholds, giving access to the UAE's lifestyle, safety, and tax benefits.

- In response to the Israel–Iran conflict, the UAE waived all visa overstay fines for Iranian nationals through December 31, 2025. This exceptional measure reflects the UAE's willingness to temporarily suspend enforcement for humanitarian reasons, though it currently applies only to Iranians.

CHAPTER 24

CIVIL LITIGATION

IN THIS CHAPTER

- Overview
- Personal Injury Claims and Related Compensation
- How to File a Civil Claim
- Service of Documents
- Statute of Limitations
- Getting Married in the UAE
- Law of the Land Hypothetical

CHAPTER 24
CIVIL LITIGATION

Overview

Civil litigation provides a mechanism for resolving disputes, ensuring that travelers have a way to seek justice if legal issues arise while visiting another country. It helps them understand their rights and obligations under local laws, which may differ from those in their home country. The civil litigation system offers a formal process for addressing conflicts, such as contract disputes or personal injury claims, and can deter unfair practices by encouraging businesses to comply with legal standards. It also allows individuals to seek financial recourse for damages or losses and helps protect them from potential exploitation by local entities. Overall, understanding civil litigation enhances a visitor's experience and safety while traveling.

Personal Injury Claims and Related Compensation[35]

The process of pursuing a personal injury claim in the United Arab Emirates begins the moment an injury occurs. Whether the harm is the result of a car accident, medical malpractice, a workplace incident, or a fall on private or public property, the first and most critical step is **to seek immediate medical attention.** The injured party should go to a licensed hospital or clinic to receive treatment and **obtain medical**

35 https://jurisprimelegal.ae/personal-injury-claims/

documentation, which will serve as key evidence in any future claim. At the same time, **the incident must be reported to the police.** A formal police report is not only essential for insurance purposes but is also a legal requirement if the injured party intends to pursue compensation through the courts. The police will investigate the incident, take witness statements, and determine who was at fault.

Once the police report and medical records are in hand, the next step is to **consult a licensed attorney** who specializes in personal injury law in the UAE. Legal representation is particularly important because the civil claims process is conducted in Arabic, and the procedures are rooted in both civil and Sharia law. The lawyer will assess whether a claim is viable and then file a case with the civil courts, typically the court of first instance in the emirate where the injury occurred. The claim must clearly state the nature of the injury, the legal grounds for liability, and the amount of compensation being sought. Supporting documentation—including the police report, medical records, employment verification for loss-of-income claims, and any witness statements—must be submitted alongside the complaint.

After the case is filed, the court may appoint a neutral expert, such as a medical examiner or financial auditor, to evaluate the extent of the injury and its impact on the victim's life. This expert assessment often plays a major role in determining the **compensation amount**. During court proceedings, both parties have the opportunity to present their arguments and submit further evidence. If the defendant is insured, the insurer will usually participate in the proceedings, as they may ultimately be responsible for paying damages.

If the court finds in favor of the injured party, it will issue a judgment awarding compensation. This compensation may include **material damages** (such as medical bills, rehabilitation costs, and lost income), **moral damages** (for pain and suffering), and in some cases, **Sharia-based diya or blood money**, especially in cases of death or permanent disability. Once a judgment is issued, the defendant (or their insurer) is legally obligated to pay the awarded amount. If the defendant fails to comply, the court may enforce the judgment through asset seizure, bank account freezes, or wage garnishment. Appeals are allowed if either party disagrees with the ruling, and the case can move up through the appellate court system, ultimately reaching the Court of Cassation if necessary. For straightforward claims, a resolution may be reached within several months, while more complex cases may take a year or more.

As a visitor to the UAE, you are fully **entitled to file a personal injury claim** and seek compensation under local laws. The UAE does not discriminate between citizens, residents, and tourists in civil court access. However, navigating the process as a foreigner can present unique challenges, especially given the language of proceedings, the need for legal representation, and the formal nature of court procedures. If you are a visitor, it is essential to report the incident to the police immediately and to obtain copies of all documentation, including hospital records, accident reports, and any witness statements. You should **also notify your embassy or consulate,** which can provide a list of approved local lawyers and sometimes assist in coordinating legal support. If you have travel insurance, **notify your provider promptly,** as many policies include coverage for legal assistance and may facilitate claims for medical expenses or liability recovery.

Your rights include the ability to pursue compensation for both financial losses and emotional or physical suffering. The UAE courts will consider the merits of your case based on evidence, not residency status. However, since many legal terms, documents, and court proceedings are conducted in Arabic, and the legal system incorporates both civil and Islamic legal principles, hiring a competent UAE-licensed attorney is strongly recommended. The court may also request your presence during hearings, though your lawyer can sometimes represent you in your absence with power of attorney.

Ultimately, the UAE legal system offers visitors meaningful legal protections and a structured process to pursue justice in the event of an injury, provided that procedural steps are followed carefully and timely.

How to File a Civil Claim

To initiate a civil case, certain requirements must be met. First, the claimant must have a valid legal interest in the matter, meaning they were directly affected by the action or inaction of the other party. Second, the claim must fall within the court's jurisdiction, which is usually determined by the location where the incident occurred, where the defendant resides or conducts business, or where the contract was executed. Additionally, there may be **time limits for filing**, depending on the type of claim—personal injury claims, for example, are generally subject to a three-year statute of limitations.

There are several types of civil claims that can be filed in UAE courts, including but not limited to **contract disputes, tort claims** (such as personal injury or defamation), **commercial claims, employment-related disputes, consumer complaints,** and **property or rental disagreements.** These cases are usually filed in the **Court of First Instance**, which has general jurisdiction over civil matters. Depending on the amount of the claim, the case may be heard in the **summary circuit** (for lower-value cases) or the **plenary circuit** (for more complex or high-value disputes).

To file a civil claim, you must prepare and submit a set of required documents. These typically include a **statement of claim** (detailing the facts of the case, legal grounds, and the amount of compensation or remedy sought), a copy of your **passport and Emirates ID** (if applicable), a **power of attorney** if you are using a legal representative, and all **supporting evidence** such as contracts, invoices, correspondence, police reports, medical records, or photographs. All documents must be translated into Arabic by a **certified legal translator** and notarized if they originate outside the UAE.

The civil claim is filed at the **Judicial Department** or **Court of First Instance** in the emirate where the defendant lives or where the dispute arose. In emirates like Abu Dhabi, Dubai, or Sharjah, this can be done electronically through the relevant judicial portal (e.g., the **Dubai Courts E-Services portal** or **Abu Dhabi Judicial Department website**). A filing fee, usually calculated as a percentage of the claim amount (often 5–7.5%), must be paid at the time of submission. After the claim is registered, the court will notify the defendant and set a hearing date. Following submission, the case proceeds through written pleadings, hearings, expert evaluations (if needed), and eventually a ruling. Parties who are not satisfied with the outcome can appeal to the **Court**

of Appeal, and ultimately to the **Court of Cassation**, although appeals must be based on points of law rather than factual disagreements.

Service of Documents[36]

Service of process in the UAE refers to the formal procedure by which a party to a legal case delivers court documents—such as a complaint, summons, or judgment—to another party to notify them of the legal action. This is a critical step in any civil case, ensuring that all parties are given proper notice and an opportunity to respond, in accordance with due process under UAE law.

The **UAE Civil Procedure Law** (**Federal Law No. 11 of 1992**, as amended) outlines how service of process must be carried out. Once a claim is filed with the competent Court of First Instance, the court is responsible for serving notice to the defendant. In most emirates, this is done through the court's **Notification Department**, which arranges for service either **in person, by registered mail**, or increasingly **through electronic means**, depending on the nature of the case and the available contact information.

For **individuals residing in the UAE**, service is typically carried out by a **court bailiff** or official process server who delivers the notice to the defendant's home or place of work. If the person cannot be located, the court may allow for alternative methods such as publishing the notice in a **local newspaper** or sending it via **email or text message**, especially when dealing with commercial disputes or entities that are difficult to reach. In cases involving **corporate entities**, the documents are usually served on the company's **registered office address** or delivered to an authorized representative. For licensed businesses, the Department of Economic Development or Free Zone Authority maintains records of business addresses and legal representatives, which the court may use to effect service.

36 https://lsp-legal.com/lsp-legal/process-server-in-the-united-arab-emirates-a-comprehensive-guide/

If the defendant is **outside the UAE**, service becomes more complex. The process must comply with **international treaties** and the rules of **judicial cooperation** between the UAE and the foreign country in question. In many cases, service is facilitated through the Ministry of Justice, which transmits the documents via the UAE embassy or consulate abroad. If there is a bilateral treaty between the UAE and the defendant's home country, that agreement will guide the procedure. Otherwise, service may occur under the **Hague Service Convention** (though the UAE is not a signatory) or through diplomatic channels.

Regardless of the method, proper service must be recorded and documented. The server must confirm the delivery, and the defendant is given a legally specified period to respond, usually between **7 and 30 days**, depending on the location and complexity of the case. Failure to respond can result in a **default judgment**.

Statute of Limitations

The statute of limitations in the United Arab Emirates refers to the legally defined time period within which a person must file a claim or initiate legal proceedings. If a case is filed after this period has expired, the court will generally reject the claim, regardless of its merits. These time limits vary depending on the nature of the case and are governed by the **UAE Civil Code** (**Federal Law No. 5 of 1985**), the **Commercial Transactions Law** (**Federal Law No. 18 of 1993**), and other specific legislation.

In **civil and personal injury cases**, as outlined in the UAE Civil Code, general limitation period is **three years** from the date the injured party becomes aware of the damage and the identity of the responsible party. However, if the injury gives rise to a **criminal offense**, such as assault, the limitation period may extend to **five years**, as per the UAE Penal Code.

For **commercial disputes**, such as unpaid debts or breach of contract between businesses, the limitation period is generally **ten years**, unless otherwise specified in the contract. This is set out under the **Commercial Transactions Law**, Federal Law No. 18 of 1993. However, shorter deadlines apply for **negotiable instruments**, such as checks and promissory notes—typically **2 to 5 years**, depending on the circumstances.

In **employment-related matters**, claims must generally be filed within **one year** of the end of the employment relationship, set out under **Federal Decree Law No. 33 of 2021 on Labor Relations.** In **real estate and construction law**, the Civil Code imposes a **ten-year "decennial liability"** for structural defects in buildings and fixed installations under Article 880. This applies to both contractors and supervising architects.

Insurance claims must usually be filed within **three years** from the date the claimant became aware of the insured event or the insurer's liability, as per the Commercial Transactions Law, while for **criminal offenses**, statutes of limitations vary. Felonies have a **20-year** limitation period, misdemeanors generally **5 years**, and minor violations **1 year**, according to the Penal Code

Overall, strict adherence to the statute of limitations is essential in the UAE, as the courts will almost always reject any claim filed after the legal deadline unless a specific legal exception applies. Given the variation in deadlines based on case type and complexity, individuals are advised to consult a UAE-licensed attorney as soon as possible to ensure timely filing.

TECHNICAL INFORMATION

Getting Married in the UAE

Getting married in the UAE is a legally recognized process that varies depending on your religion, nationality, and residency status. **For Muslims**—whether Emirati or expatriate—the marriage process is governed by Islamic (Sharia) law and **must be formalized through the Sharia courts.** The requirements include the presence of the bride's father or legal guardian, two male Muslim witnesses, and a mandatory pre-marital medical screening conducted at a government-approved clinic. Both the bride and groom must be at least 18 years old. If the bride has been previously married, she must provide documentation such as a divorce certificate or a death certificate of her former spouse. Muslim couples typically formalize their marriage through the Sharia Court in their emirate of residence, such as the Dubai Courts or the Abu Dhabi Judicial Department.

For **non-Muslim** couples, the process has become significantly easier with the introduction of **civil marriage** in Abu Dhabi. In 2021, Abu Dhabi implemented reforms that allow non-Muslim residents and tourists to legally marry through a secular process overseen by the **Abu Dhabi Civil Family Court.** This type of marriage does not require a religious ceremony, witnesses, or the presence of a guardian. Couples—whether tourists or residents—can apply for a civil marriage using their passports and, if applicable, Emirates IDs. They must also provide proof of marital status, such as a certificate of singleness or a divorce decree. While a medical test is optional, the entire process is highly efficient and often completed within 24 to 48 hours. Applications can be submitted online through the Abu Dhabi Judicial Department at https://www.adjd.gov.ae.

Some foreign nationals may also be eligible to marry at their respective embassies or consulates within the UAE. This option depends entirely on the laws of the individual's home country. Countries such as the United Kingdom, France, India, Russia, and the Philippines generally permit marriage through their diplomatic missions, but requirements, fees, and scheduling vary. In contrast, the United States **does not** perform marriages at its embassy; American citizens must marry through UAE courts.

For couples who prefer a symbolic or religious wedding ceremony—such as those held at churches, Hindu temples, or hotels—it is important to understand that these are **not legally binding** on their own. A religious or symbolic ceremony must be followed by official registration either through a court or an embassy to be recognized under UAE law. Once the marriage is completed and a legal certificate is issued, couples may need to have the document attested if they plan to use it outside the UAE. This involves a multi-step process: the marriage certificate must first be attested by the UAE Ministry of Justice, then legalized by the UAE Ministry of Foreign Affairs and International Cooperation (MOFA) and finally authenticated by the home country's embassy if required. Details for MOFA services are available at https://www.mofa.gov.ae.

It is important to note that **same-sex marriage is not recognized in the UAE.** The country adheres to Islamic law, under which same-sex relationships are

Law of the Land Hypothetical

HYPOTHETICAL: *Julia, a 34-year-old French tourist visiting Abu Dhabi, slips and falls in the lobby of a luxury hotel due to a recently mopped floor that had no warning signs posted. She suffers a fractured wrist and incurs $5,000 USD in medical expenses at a private hospital. The hotel management apologizes but refuses to offer compensation. As a non-resident foreign tourist, does Julia have the right to file a personal injury claim against the hotel in the UAE, and if so, what steps must she take to initiate civil litigation?*

ANSWER: **Yes.** *Julia has the full legal right to file a personal injury claim in the UAE, even as a foreign visitor. The UAE legal system does not restrict access to civil courts based on citizenship or residency status. Under Federal Law No. 5 of 1985 (UAE Civil Code), individuals may seek compensation if they have suffered harm due to another party's negligence. The hotel's failure to post a warning sign for a wet floor may be considered a breach of its duty of care toward guests, which can form the legal basis for liability in tort (Articles 282–292 of the Civil Code). Julia must gather evidence, including medical records, photos (if available), and any hotel or police reports. Although she is no longer in the country, she can appoint a UAE-licensed lawyer through a notarized power of attorney to represent her. Her lawyer would file the claim with the Abu Dhabi Court of First Instance, submit Arabic-translated documents, and pay the filing fee (around 5% of the claim amount).*

The statute of limitations for personal injury in the UAE is **three years**. *If the court finds the hotel liable, Julia may be awarded compensation*

for medical expenses and emotional distress. Being a tourist does not prevent her from pursuing legal action in the UAE.

CHAPTER 25

OTHER THINGS TO KNOW

IN THIS CHAPTER

- Tourists and Street Hustling
- Safety Concerns and Practical Tips
- In the Event of Death
- Experiencing Financial Hardship

CHAPTER 25

OTHER THINGS TO KNOW

Tourists and Street Hustling

Street hustling is not common in the UAE, particularly when compared to other tourist-heavy regions. The United Arab Emirates—especially cities like Dubai and Abu Dhabi—maintains strict public order laws, high surveillance, and a significant police presence, which make overt forms of street hustling (such as aggressive solicitation, scams, or unlicensed street sales) relatively rare. That said, **some low-level forms of hustling do occur**, particularly in crowded tourist areas, but they are more discreet and often involve gray-market activity rather than outright scams.

For example, in parts of **Old Dubai** (**Deira, Al Fahidi, or near the Gold Souk**), some street vendors or touts may approach tourists offering counterfeit goods, cheap watches, or knock-off designer handbags. You might also encounter people promoting unlicensed tour packages, massage services, or discounted electronics. These individuals are usually persistent but not aggressive, and local authorities periodically conduct crackdowns on such activity. In high-end districts like Downtown Dubai or the Marina, such solicitation is almost nonexistent due to heavy policing and CCTV surveillance.

For tourists, the impact is usually minimal—but it's important to **stay alert and exercise caution**. Buying from unauthorized sellers may result in low-quality or fake products and engaging with unlicensed services can lead to legal issues or personal safety risks. Some tourists have also reported being overcharged or misled about the nature of goods or services.

The UAE takes consumer protection seriously, and tourists who feel harassed or defrauded can contact the local police or the **Dubai Department of Economy and Tourism** (**DED**) or similar authorities in other emirates. Reporting incidents is easy, and complaints are often acted upon swiftly, especially if there's evidence such as a photo or video.

Safety Concerns and Practical Tips

While street hustling is not widespread in the UAE, some safety concerns may still arise from interactions with unauthorized vendors or overly persistent solicitors in tourist-heavy areas like Deira, the Gold Souk, or parts of Al Fahidi. The main risks for tourists include being overcharged, sold fake merchandise, or unknowingly violating local laws by engaging with unlicensed operators. In some cases, tourists may feel uncomfortable due to repeated or overly pushy solicitation, even though such behavior rarely escalates to physical threats.

To protect themselves, tourists should **avoid engaging** with anyone who approaches them unsolicited in public markets or streets. A polite but **firm "No, thank you"** is usually sufficient, and continuing to walk away without stopping helps signal disinterest. Tourists should never hand over money, passports, or phones to strangers offering to "help" or show them something. It's also best to purchase goods and services from reputable, licensed shops or stalls and to book tours, transportation, or spa services through official platforms or hotel concierge services. Keeping valuables secure, avoiding carrying large amounts of cash, and being mindful of surroundings—especially in crowded areas—are all practical precautions.

Culturally, the UAE places a high value on respectful and composed public behavior. Tourists should avoid shouting, gesturing aggressively, or insulting hustlers, as such actions could violate local laws on public decency and be taken very seriously. Instead, maintaining calm body language, dressing modestly in traditional markets, and speaking respectfully—even when declining offers—can help avoid misunderstandings. If a hustler becomes insistent or follows a tourist, it's acceptable to alert nearby security or police officers, who are generally approachable and responsive.

In essence, while the risk posed by street hustlers in the UAE is low compared to other countries, a combination of vigilance, respectful disengagement, and use of official vendors will help ensure a safe and hassle-free experience.

In the Event of Death

In the event of a death while visiting the United Arab Emirates, the situation is treated with seriousness, legal formality, and respect for the deceased and their family. When a foreign national dies—whether from natural causes, an accident, or other circumstances—the first step is to **notify the local police immediately.** The authorities will secure the area and launch an initial investigation to confirm the cause and circumstances of the death. The deceased is then transported to a government hospital, where the Emergency and Forensic Medicine Department will issue an official death notification. If the death is sudden, unexplained, or involves any suspicion of foul play, a forensic autopsy may be required, and the Public Prosecution may initiate a legal review. This process must be completed before the body can be released for burial or repatriation.

A death certificate will be issued in Arabic once the police investigation is closed and the hospital confirms the cause of death. If the family intends to use this certificate abroad, it must be translated into English or another relevant language and attested by the UAE Ministry of Health and Prevention, the Ministry of Foreign Affairs, and the deceased's embassy or consulate. The embassy plays a critical role throughout the process, serving as a liaison between UAE authorities and the deceased's family. Consular officials help notify the next of kin, assist with document processing, and coordinate funeral or repatriation arrangements according to the family's wishes.

If the body is to be **repatriated** to the home country, the family must appoint a licensed funeral services provider in the UAE to manage the logistics. This includes preparing the body for transport, securing a sealed casket, and obtaining all necessary permits. Airlines require several official documents to accept the body as cargo, including the death certificate, embalming certificate, a no-objection certificate from the consulate, the police report, and the deceased's passport. The consulate will issue a consular mortuary certificate once all formalities are complete, clearing the way for international transport.

If the family opts for burial in the UAE, this is allowed with government and embassy approval. Non-Muslims may be buried in designated cemeteries, such as those located in Jebel Ali in Dubai or Al Bateen in Abu Dhabi. Religious services can be held in accordance with the deceased's beliefs, provided they comply with UAE regulations. Funeral homes and religious institutions in the country are experienced in handling such multicultural arrangements. If the deceased had **travel insurance**, the insurer should be notified as soon as possible. Many policies cover the costs associated with repatriation or local burial. To make a claim, the insurance company will typically require certified copies of the death certificate and other official documents.

Though the experience is emotionally and logistically overwhelming, the UAE has clear procedures in place for managing the death of a foreign national. Embassies, hospitals, and funeral service providers are accustomed to working together to support families during such difficult times. Tourists are encouraged to travel with comprehensive insurance and to have their emergency contact information accessible, as consulates serve as the primary point of support in these tragic circumstances.

Experiencing Financial Hardship

Experiencing financial hardship while traveling in the United Arab Emirates can be challenging, especially for tourists who may be unfamiliar with the local laws and support systems. If a traveler runs out of funds or faces unexpected expenses such as medical emergencies, accommodation issues, or lost belongings, they may find themselves in a difficult situation. Unlike some countries that provide extensive social safety nets for visitors, **the UAE expects travelers to be financially self-sufficient during their stay.**

In the event of financial difficulty, the first step is to **contact your country's embassy or consulate**. Many embassies can offer limited assistance, such as helping you communicate with family or friends to arrange for emergency funds or providing information about local charitable organizations. However, embassies generally cannot provide direct financial aid or cover debts incurred while traveling. Travelers should also reach out to their **travel insurance provider**, if they have one, as many policies include coverage for emergency cash advances, medical care, or trip interruption.

It is important for travelers to avoid incurring debts they cannot repay, as the UAE has strict laws regarding unpaid bills, including for hotels, taxis, and medical services. Non-payment can lead to legal action, including fines, travel bans, or even detention in some cases. If a traveler anticipates they may not be able to pay, they should communicate openly with service providers or hotels to negotiate payment plans or seek alternative arrangements.

Some charitable organizations and community groups, such as **Emirates Red Crescent**, provide **limited support** to foreigners facing hardship, but this assistance is generally modest and not guaranteed. Travelers are advised to plan ahead by securing sufficient funds, having access to emergency credit, and purchasing comprehensive travel insurance that covers unexpected costs.

Overall, while the UAE is a safe and well-organized destination, financial hardship during travel can become complicated due to strict legal and financial regulations. Tourists facing such difficulties should act promptly by seeking help from their embassy and insurance company, avoiding unpaid debts, and exploring any available local support resources.

CHAPTER 26

QUICK REFERENCE GUIDE

IN THIS CHAPTER

- Quick Chapter References to Important Topics

CHAPTER 26

QUICK REFERENCE GUIDE

Crime in the UAE

Are there particular areas I should avoid as a tourist?

No. Crime rates in the UAE are generally very low, and there are no specific areas that tourists are commonly advised to avoid. The country maintains strict law enforcement and high public safety standards, making most parts of cities like Dubai and Abu Dhabi safe for visitors. However, like in any major city worldwide, it's wise to stay alert and exercise common-sense precautions, especially in crowded places or at night. *For more details, see Chapter 3.*

Drug Offenses

Is the possession of marijuana legal?

No. Possession of marijuana is **illegal** in the UAE, and the country enforces a strict zero-tolerance policy. Even small amounts or traces on personal items can lead to arrest, imprisonment, fines, and deportation for foreigners. Security checks at airports include drug tests, and testing positive—regardless of where the drug was used—can result in legal action. Travelers should avoid bringing any marijuana or related substances into the UAE to prevent serious consequences.

Is the possession of cocaine legal?

No. Possession of cocaine is **illegal** in the UAE. Under Federal Law No. 14 of 1995, the UAE enforces a strict zero-tolerance policy toward all narcotics, including cocaine. Even trace amounts found in personal items or bodily fluids can result in severe penalties. *For more details, see Chapter 4.*

Alcohol-Related Offenses

What is the legal drinking age?

The legal drinking age in the United Arab Emirates is **21 years old.** This applies across all emirates, including Dubai and Abu Dhabi. Individuals under 21 are not allowed to purchase, possess, or consume alcohol. Selling or providing alcohol to someone underage is prohibited and can lead to penalties such as imprisonment and fines up to 100,000 AED (approximately USD 27,200). Sellers who verify the buyer's age with official ID are generally not held liable.

What is the legal blood alcohol limit?

In the UAE, the legal blood alcohol concentration (BAC) limit for driving is **0.00%.** This means that any detectable amount of alcohol in your system while operating a vehicle is considered an offense. Unlike many countries that permit a certain BAC level, the UAE enforces a **strict zero-tolerance policy**. Even minute amounts can lead to severe penalties, including fines, imprisonment, license suspension, and in some cases, deportation for foreign nationals. *For more details, see Chapter 5.*

Firearm & Ammunition Offenses

Can I possess a gun?

No. Possessing a gun in the UAE is strictly prohibited for tourists and most expatriates without a special license. Firearms can only be legally owned by UAE citizens or certain professionals under strict conditions. Bringing a firearm into the country without authorization can lead to severe penalties, including imprisonment and deportation. Tourists should never attempt to carry or import guns while in the UAE.

Can I possess ammunition?

No. Possessing ammunition in the UAE without explicit authorization is illegal. Federal Decree Law No. 17 of 2019 prohibits the possession, acquisition, importation, exportation, or transit of weapons and ammunition without a valid license issued by the Ministry of Interior. This applies to all individuals, including tourists. Attempting to bring ammunition into the country without proper authorization can lead to severe penalties. Even possessing ammunition for legitimate purposes, such as hunting, is not permitted without prior approval from the relevant authorities. Travelers should refrain from carrying any form of ammunition when visiting the UAE to avoid legal complications. *For more details, see Chapter 6.*

Prostitution

Is prostitution legal?

No. Prostitution is strictly illegal in the UAE, including Dubai and Abu Dhabi. Engaging in, promoting, or facilitating prostitution—whether in person or online—can lead to severe legal consequences. Penalties include **imprisonment, heavy fines,** and **deportation** for foreign nationals. The UAE enforces a **zero-tolerance policy toward prostitution**, and authorities actively monitor and prosecute related activities. Even private arrangements or online solicitations can result in criminal charges. Given the stringent laws and enforcement, it is strongly advised to avoid any involvement in prostitution-related activities while in the UAE. *For more details, see Chapter 7.*

LGBTQ

Is homosexuality legal?

No. Homosexuality is **illegal** in the UAE, with consensual same-sex activity punishable by imprisonment—up to 14 years in Abu Dhabi and 10 years in Dubai. The laws are based on interpretations of Sharia and can theoretically carry harsher penalties, though these are rarely enforced.

Are same sex public displays of affection socially acceptable?

No. Same-sex public displays of affection are **not socially acceptable** in the UAE and can lead to legal consequences. The country maintains conservative cultural norms rooted in Islamic tradition, and public affection—even between heterosexual couples—is generally discouraged. For same-sex couples, holding hands, hugging, or kissing in public can attract unwanted attention, result in complaints, and potentially lead to arrest, fines, or deportation. LGBTQ+ travelers are strongly advised to avoid any public behavior that may be perceived as romantic or intimate to stay within the bounds of both social expectations and the law. *For more details, see Chapter 8.*

Arrested in the UAE

Would I be entitled to bail if I'm arrested?

Yes. You may be entitled to bail in the UAE, depending on the nature of the offense. For minor or non-violent crimes, bail can be granted by the police, prosecutor, or court. It may require a passport deposit, a financial bond, or other conditions like a travel ban. However, bail is not allowed for serious offenses such as those punishable by life imprisonment or death. A local lawyer can help apply for bail, but embassies cannot influence the decision.

Will a lawyer be provided to me if I cannot afford one?

Yes. If you cannot afford a lawyer in the UAE, **free legal aid is available**, especially for civil, family, and certain criminal matters. Service eligibility is determined by your income and the seriousness of your case. *For more details, see Chapter 10.*

Helping a Friend or Relative Imprisoned in the UAE

Can I send money to a friend or family member imprisoned in the UAE?

Yes. You can send money to a friend or family member imprisoned in the UAE, but the method depends on the prison. In Dubai and Abu Dhabi, cash deposits are allowed on specific days. Some prisons, like Abu Dhabi Federal Prison, only accept transfers via the Ministry of Interior app. In Ajman and other emirates, inmates may receive funds through official apps or into digital canteen accounts. Rules vary, so it's important to check with the specific facility or consult the inmate's embassy for guidance.

Can I remain in the UAE upon release from prison or jail after my sentence is complete?

No. If you're a foreign national, you will most likely be deported after completing a prison sentence in the UAE. Courts often issue judicial deportation orders for serious crimes, and even without a conviction, administrative deportation can occur for reasons of public safety or morality. While it's possible to appeal or request a waiver in rare cases, remaining in the UAE after release is generally not allowed unless special legal approval is granted. *For more details, see Chapter 12.*

Crime Victim Assistance

Can a victim of a crime be legally compensated?

Yes. Victims of crime in the UAE can be legally compensated, especially if they suffer physical, emotional, or financial harm. Compensation may be awarded through the **criminal court** as part of sentencing or by filing a **civil lawsuit** for damages under the UAE Civil Code. For violent crimes or serious injuries, victims may receive court-ordered restitution from the offender. In cases involving unknown or insolvent offenders, compensation may be limited, but some emirates, such as Dubai and Abu Dhabi, have **government-backed victim support programs** that may offer assistance.

Does the UAE government offer assistance for family members of homicide victims?

Yes. The UAE government provides support for families of homicide victims through laws and specialized programs. The Family Protection Policy and Federal Law No. 10 of 2019 establish legal protections and access to social services, including restraining orders and counseling. Police departments like Dubai Police offer Victim Support Programs that assist with legal guidance, medical referrals, and emotional support. Shelters such as the Dubai Foundation for Women and Children also provide safe accommodation and counseling. These combined efforts ensure families receive legal aid, emotional care, and protection. *For more details, see Chapter 14.*

U.S. Consulate Assistance

Are there any limitations to the consulate assistance I can receive while in the UAE?

Yes. Consulate assistance in the UAE is helpful but limited. They cannot offer legal advice, however they can help replace lost passports, contact family, and support you during emergencies. However, they cannot intervene in legal cases, provide lawyers or pay legal fees, secure release from detention, or offer financial aid except in rare emergencies. Their help must follow UAE laws and depends on the consulate's resources. *For more details, see Chapter 14.*

Police

Is there an official police force?

Yes. The UAE has an official police force. Each emirate has its own police department responsible for maintaining law and order, enforcing laws, and ensuring public safety. The Abu Dhabi Police and Dubai Police are the most well-known among them. These forces work alongside federal security agencies to provide comprehensive policing across the country. *For more details, see Chapter 15.*

How to Get Legal Help in the UAE

Is there a resource in the UAE to find legal representation?

Yes. In the UAE you can find legal representation through several resources. The **UAE Bar Association** is the primary organization that can help connect you with licensed lawyers. Many emirates also have legal aid centers or government-sponsored services that assist those who cannot afford private lawyers. Additionally, embassies and consulates sometimes provide lists of local attorneys for their nationals.

Is there free legal representation assistance?

Yes. The UAE offers free legal assistance in certain cases, mainly for those who cannot afford a lawyer. This is often provided through government legal aid programs or legal aid centers in some emirates. The availability and scope can vary, usually focusing on criminal defense or specific civil matters. Foreigners can sometimes access this help, but it depends on the case and local regulations. *For more details, see Chapter 16.*

Foreign Embassies in the UAE

Where can I find a complete and updated list of all diplomatic missions in the UAE?

You can find a comprehensive and up-to-date list of all diplomatic missions in the UAE through the Ministry of Foreign Affairs and International Cooperation (MoFAIC) at https://www.mofa.gov.ae/en/missions/foreign-missions-in-uae. Their official directory includes contact details and locations for embassies and consulates in both Abu Dhabi and Dubai.

Where is the U.S. Embassy in the UAE located?

The U.S. Embassy in the UAE is located in **Abu Dhabi at Plot 38, Sector W59-02, Street No. 4, Embassies District, Airport Road at Rabdan.** The U.S. also has a Consulate General in Dubai at the corner of **Al Seef Road and Sheikh Khalifa bin Zayed Road, Umm Hurair First.** Both provide consular services like visa processing, passport renewal, and emergency help. *For more details, see Chapter 16.*

Medical Facilities & Hospitals

Is there a number I can call for ambulance and fire emergencies?

Yes. In the UAE you can call **998** for ambulance emergencies and **997** for fire emergencies. These numbers work nationwide, including in Abu Dhabi and Dubai.

If I am injured while on vacation in the UAE, are there hospitals that are recommended for tourists?

Yes. The UAE has many reputable hospitals that welcome tourists. In Dubai, popular choices include Rashid Hospital, Mediclinic City Hospital, and American Hospital Dubai. Abu Dhabi offers Cleveland Clinic Abu Dhabi and NMC Royal Hospital. These hospitals have good emergency care and often provide services in English. It's best to check if your travel insurance is accepted. *For more details, see Chapter 17.*

Driving in the UAE

Which side of the road do I drive on?

You drive on **the right side** of the road in the UAE.

Can I use my driver's license from my home country to drive in the UAE?

Yes. You can use your foreign driver's license to drive in the UAE for a limited time, usually **up to six months**. After that, you may need to get a UAE driver's license, which sometimes requires passing tests depending on your home country. It's best to check the specific rules based on your nationality.

How old do I need to be to rent a car?

You typically need to be **at least 21 years old** to rent a car in the UAE, though some rental companies may require drivers to be 23 or older. Additionally, a valid driver's license held for at least one year is usually required. *For more details, see Chapter 18.*

Nude Beaches & Clothing-Optional Resorts

Is public nudity legal on the beaches?

No. Public nudity is **illegal** on UAE beaches. Non-revealing swimwear is allowed in designated areas but must be worn properly. Topless sunbathing and nudity can lead to fines, imprisonment, or deportation. In some emirates like Sharjah, dress codes are even stricter. It's best to dress modestly and follow local rules. *For more details, see Chapter 19.*

Tourist Taxation

Is there a room tax in the UAE?

Yes. The UAE imposes a room tax, often called a "tourism fee" or "municipality fee," on hotel stays. It's usually a small daily charge per room, varying by emirate and hotel rating. This fee is added to your bill when you check out.

Is there any fee associated with leaving the UAE by air?

Yes. There is a departure fee when flying out of the UAE. Dubai charges about 75 AED (about $21 USD), Sharjah about 35 AED (about $10 USD), and Abu Dhabi currently has no departure fee. These fees are usually included in your airline ticket. *For more details, see Chapter 22.*

Long-Term Stays

Do I need to return to my home country to apply for a work permit in the UAE?

No. You don't have to leave the UAE to apply for a work permit. If you're already in the country, your employer can change your visa status to a work permit without you returning home. If you're outside, your employer can apply for an entry visa so you can come and complete the work permit process.

As an American, how long can I stay in the UAE without a visa?

As a U.S. citizen, you can stay in the UAE visa-free for up to **30 days**, with a passport valid for at least six months and a confirmed onward ticket. You can apply for a 30-day visa extension while in the country, though approval is at the immigration authorities' discretion. *For more details, see Chapter 23.*

In the Event of Death

What documents would an embassy need regarding the death of a tourist?

An embassy typically requires the tourist's passport, death certificate issued by local authorities, and any medical or police reports related to the death. They may also ask for proof of relationship from family members handling the case and any relevant travel documents. These help the embassy assist with repatriation and other formalities. *For more details, see Chapter 25.*

EMERGENCY/IMPORTANT CONTACT NUMBERS IN THE UAE

Please consider putting some of these numbers in your phone **prior** to traveling to the UAE.

Emergency Numbers:

- **Police:** 999
- **Fire Department:** 997
- **Ambulance:** 998
- **Civil Defense (for accidents, disasters):** 997
- **Electricity & Water Emergency (DEWA - Dubai):** 991

Other Useful Contacts:

- **General Emergency (Unified Hotline):** 999
- **Tourist Police (Dubai):** 800 4438
- **Coast Guard / Sea Rescue:** 996
- **Roadside Assistance (Dubai Police Non-Emergency):** 901
- **RTA (Roads & Transport Authority – Dubai):** 800 9090
- **Public Transport Customer Care (Abu Dhabi):** 800 88888

- **Sharjah Transport Hotline:** 600 525252

Medical Assistance:

- **Ministry of Health & Prevention (MOHAP):** 800 11111
- **Dubai Health Authority (DHA):** 800 342 (800 DHA)
- **Abu Dhabi Health Services (SEHA):** 800 50
- **24/7 Dubai Ambulance Service:** 998

Embassy & Consular Assistance:

- **U.S. Embassy (Abu Dhabi):** +971 2 414 2200
- **U.S. Consulate (Dubai):** +971 4 309 4000
- **British Embassy (Abu Dhabi):** +971 2 610 1100
- **Canadian Embassy (Abu Dhabi):** +971 2 694 0300
- **List of all embassies/consulates in UAE:** https://www.usembassy.gov; search by country and "UAE"

Legal Assistance:

- **UAE Bar Association:** https://www.uaebar.ae
- **Legal Aid – Abu Dhabi Judicial Department:** https://www.adjd.gov.ae
- **Dubai Courts Legal Services Directory:** https://www.dc.gov.ae

Other Importance Hotlines:

- **Consumer Protection Hotline:** 600 522 225
- **Human Rights Department (Dubai Police):** 800 5005
- **Islamic Affairs & Charitable Activities (Prayer/Religious Info):** 800 600

USEFUL ARABIC PHRASES

Greetings

HI/HELLO – مرحباً (Marhaban)

GOOD MORNING – صباح الخير (Sabah al-khayr)

GOOD AFTERNOON – مساء الخير (Masa' al-khayr)

GOOD NIGHT – تصبح على خير (Tusbih 'ala khayr)

GOODBYE – مع السلامة (Ma'a al-salamah)

Magic Words

PLEASE – من فضلك (Min fadlik [to female], Min fadlak [to male])

THANK YOU – شكراً (Shukran)

YOU'RE WELCOME – على الرحب والسعة (Ala al-rahb wa al-sa'a) or عفواً ('Afwan)

CHEERS! – في صحتك! (Fi sihhatik!)

EXCUSE ME – عفواً ('Afwan) or لو سمحت (Law samaht)

Getting Around

WHERE IS THE BATHROOM? – أين الحمام؟ (Ayna al-hammam?)

WHAT TIME IS IT? – كم الساعة؟ (Kam al-sa'ah?)

HOW DO I GET TO…? – فـيك لصأ ىلإ…؟ (Kayfa asil ila...?)

WHERE DOES THIS TRAIN/BUS GO? – ىلإ نيأ بـهذي اذه راطقلا / صابلا؟ (Ila ayna yadhhab hatha al-qitar / al-bas?)

RESTAURANT – معطم (Mat'am)

HOW MUCH DOES THIS COST? – مك رعس اذه؟ (Kam si'r hatha?)

TRAIN/METRO STATION – ةطحم راطقلا / ورتملا (Mahattat al-qitar / al-metro)

Communication

DO YOU SPEAK ENGLISH? – له ثدحتت ملكتت ةيزيلجنإلا؟ (Hal tatakallam al-Ingleeziyah?)

I DO NOT UNDERSTAND – ال مهفأ (La afham)

I DON'T SPEAK (COUNTRY'S LANGUAGE) – ال ملكتأ ةيـبرعلا (La atakallam al-'Arabiyah)

I DON'T KNOW – ال فـرعأ (La a'rif)

Emergency

HELP! – ةدجنلا! (Al-najdah!)

CALL AN AMBULANCE! – لصتا فاعسإلاب! (Ittasil bil-is'aaf!)

I NEED A DOCTOR – جاتحأ ىلإ بـيـبط (Ahtaj ila tabeeb)

POLICE – ةطرشلا (Al-shurtah)

I'M LOST – انأ هئات / ةهئات (Ana taeih [male] / taeihah [female])

IT'S AN EMERGENCY – اهنإ ةلاح ةئراط (Innaha halah taree'ah)

GLOSSARY

ACQUITTAL: A jury verdict that a criminal defendant is not guilty, or the finding of a judge that the evidence cannot support a conviction.

ADVERSARY PROCEEDING: A lawsuit arising from a controversy that begins with filing a complaint.

AFFIDAVIT: A written statement made under oath.

APPEAL: A request made after a trial court has decided against one party in which the losing party asks a higher court to review the decision for legal error.

ARRAIGNMENT: A proceeding in which a criminal defendant is brought to court, told of the charges, and asked to plead guilty or not guilty.

BAIL: The temporary release of a person from jail when awaiting trial, on condition that a sum of money be lodged or deposited to guarantee an appearance in court.

BARRISTER: A lawyer admitted to plead at the Bar and who may try cases in superior court.

BURDEN OF PROOF: The duty to prove disputed facts.

CAUSE OF ACTION: A legal claim in a civil action.

COMPLAINT: A written statement that begins a civil lawsuit in which the plaintiff details the claims.

CONTRACT: An agreement between two or more persons to do something or to not do something.

CONVICTION: A judgment of guilt against a person charged with a crime.

CUSTOMS DUTY: A tariff or tax imposed on goods when transported across international borders.

COURT LIAISON: A person that coordinates with attorneys to perform administrative duties, such as scheduling witnesses, sharing information with law enforcement, and overseeing the reporting of cases to foreign embassies when applicable.

DAMAGES: Money that a defendant pays to a plaintiff in a civil case if the plaintiff wins.

DEFENDANT: 1) The individual against whom a civil claim is filed; 2) The individual against whom a criminal claim is filed.

FELONY: A serious crime, punishable by more than one year in prison.

MAGISTRATE: A judicial officer of a district court, who conducts initial proceedings in criminal cases, decides criminal misdemeanor cases, conducts many pretrial civil and criminal matters on behalf of district judges, and decides civil cases with the consent of the parties.

MISDEMEANOR: An offense punishable by one year or less in jail.

PLAINTIFF: A person or business that files a formal complaint with the court.

PLEA: In a criminal case, the answer of "guilty," "not guilty," or "no contest" in response to a criminal charge.

SOLICITOR: A lawyer who advises clients, represents them in lower court, and prepares cases for barristers to try in higher courts.

SOVEREIGN IMMUNITY: A legal doctrine by which the sovereign or the state (i.e. government) cannot commit a legal wrong and thus, it is immune from criminal and civil liability and cannot be sued.

STATUTE: A written law passed by a legislative body.

STATUTE OF LIMITATIONS: A statute prescribing a period of limitation to bring certain types of legal actions. If the action is not brought within that time, the person or entity (in a criminal context) is permanently barred from suing in court.

SUBPOENA: A command, issued under court authority, for a witness to appear and to give testimony.

TESTIMONY: Evidence presented orally by witnesses.

VERDICT: The decision of a judge or jury in a case.

WARRANT: Court authorization to conduct a search or to make an arrest.

ACKNOWLEDGMENTS

This book series would never have seen the light of day without the able assistance of the following people:

Kathy Adams, my paralegal for over 22 years, who is the "Best" I've ever worked with during my entire legal career because of her amazing work ethic, organizational skills, and her ability to think outside of the box in unique and creative ways;

Ally Knez-Siddique, a professional writer, and one of my paralegals, whose eye for detail, according to her, is both a blessing and a curse;

Gino Ibanez, my former law clerk, whose exceptional research skills helped move this book along in its early stages;

Rosa Diaz Graham, my legal assistant who helped with research and word processing at the very beginning of this project;

Shelia Martin, one of my former paralegals, worked diligently on this series of books, even after taking on another job. Her organizational skills are reflected throughout;

Mindy Scarlett, my marketing and publishing "Guru"! Her creativity and vision have no boundaries!

ABOUT THE AUTHOR

Michael L. Moore practices in Orlando, Florida, the city where he spent his formative years. He credits the trauma of having his brother murdered when he was only 10 years old, as the catalyst that drew him into the practice of law.

Moore attended Florida State University, where he was a member of the FSU debate team. Upon graduating, he was awarded a full scholarship to attend the University of Tennessee College of Law, where he was elected President of the Student Bar Association. He further honed his advocacy and public speaking skills by participating in 'moot court' competitions.

After clerking at the Tennessee Attorney General's office while in law school, Moore moved back to Orlando, Florida, to work at the State Attorney's Office as a prosecutor, and where he was fortunate enough to meet the young lady that would eventually become his wife. Moore moved on to working for private law firms, both local and national, and eventually established his own law firm in 1999. He continues to make Orlando his home base.

It was the murder of a close friend and client in Jamaica that caused Moore to realize that books on laws in other countries were few and far between, and he was inspired to create Law of the Land Publishing. Moore launched Law of the Land Publishing to provide a series of guidebooks and a membership site for tourists and business travelers to stay up to date on the laws in each country they travel to, as well as having access to assistance if they run into legal issues.

"My vision is to educate people on what their legal rights are, and how they can access legal assistance, no matter where they have to travel to in the world," said Moore. "As Americans, we have a right to due process, but in some countries, you don't even have the right to access a square meal when incarcerated. My goal is to provide the information needed to stay out of trouble, as well as having access to assistance if trouble finds you."